PANDEMICS, PLAGUES, AND NATURAL DISASTERS

What Is **GOD** *Saying to Us?*

Erwin W. Lutzer

MOODY PUBLISHERS

CHICAGO

Library of Congress Control Number: 2020911246

ISBN: 978-0-8024-2345-0

All websites and phone numbers listed herein are accurate at the time of publication but may change in the future or cease to exist. The listing of website references and resources does not imply publisher endorsement of the site's entire contents. Groups and organizations are listed for informational purposes, and listing does not imply publisher endorsement of their activities.

Originally delivered by fleets of horse-drawn wagons, the affordable paperbacks from D. L. Moody's publishing house resourced the church and served everyday people. Now, after more than 125 years of publishing and ministry, Moody Publishers' mission remains the same—even if our delivery systems have changed a bit. For more information on other books (and resources) created from a biblical perspective, go to www.moodypublishers.com or write to:

Moody Publishers
820 N. LaSalle Boulevard
Chicago, IL 60610

1 3 5 7 9 10 8 6 4 2

Printed in the United States of America

PANDEMICS, PLAGUES, AND NATURAL DISASTERS

In loving memory of Anna DeJong,
who was swept away in the DuPage River,
which had swollen its banks due to heavy rains.
Downstream she was caught by the loving arms
of her heavenly Father.
"The eternal God is your dwelling place,
and underneath are the everlasting arms."
(Deuteronomy 33:27a)

13 Sept 2020

Pastor John
You are a blessing,
enjoyment retirement and
we know God continues for
you & Debbie to follow
Jesus and share His love
to all. Shalom,
Edward & Carolyn Brooker

CONTENTS

CHAPTER 1

THE CRISIS THAT CHANGED EVERYTHING

COVID-19 is the pandemic that changed everything. The "new normal" will not be the same as the "old normal." For years to come we will talk about BC (Before COVID) and AC (After COVID). *Normal* may never come back.

This virus, originating in Wuhan, China, soon spread around the globe. In a matter of months, the United States led the other countries in having the largest number of deaths. In response to the mandates of our political leadership, the nation went into lockdown. Cars lined up for miles at food banks and unemployment numbers skyrocketed.

Every country of the world experienced hardship and panic.

Reports from India described the horrible plight of day workers, now forced to walk back home without food and water, many dying along the way. The jobs that supplied money for their families ended, leaving them destitute, with grinding poverty, and no means of keeping themselves and their families alive. A friend of mine who lives in India reported that what little money some had was spent in liquor stores, which were deemed "essential businesses" while many other "nonessential businesses" were in lockdown.

Many countries in Europe suffered greatly. England was effectively shut down, even as the country's own prime minister contracted the virus and thanked the medical community for saving his life. I have friends in Albania who said that they were not permitted to leave their homes without tapping an app on their smartphones and getting permission. Church members along with other people from the community were delivering whatever available food there was to those who were starving. Yes, at the writing of this, things are changing, restrictions are being relaxed, but slowly.

Name the country, and COVID-19 was wreaking havoc there. All tried to respond as best they could. Throughout the world, each death—whether of a parent, grandparent, brother, or sister—represented a family. Here in the United States, relatives were often denied close contact with the dying; many, especially of the older generation, died alone, unable to say goodbye to their loved ones.

As if there wasn't enough grief in our country, at the height of the COVID-19 pandemic, dozens of tornadoes swept though some of our southern states, destroying neighborhoods, flattening homes, and killing dozens. In some instances, a parent was killed and their children lived; many families suffered losses of one kind or another along with their livelihoods. All the while COVID-19 added to their woes and held entire communities in fear.

As parents throughout the country lost their jobs and desperately began the search for unemployment benefits, they wondered what they should tell their children. Would there be food on the table? Tens of thousands, and eventually millions, were tested to see if they had the virus. Thankfully, most did not, but those who did felt as if COVID-19 was a death sentence. And for some, it was.

Churches transitioned from actual meetings to "virtual services" online. Giving decreased in some churches, and some Christian ministries haven't survived. My greatest heartbreak is for those international gospel preaching ministries that are almost totally dependent on American funds. Fear has caused many Christians to pull back their giving; some because of genuine financial need, others because of our tendency to hoard our assets, keeping more than we need.

As states "opened up," businesses reopened with new restrictions, new policies, and continuing fears. Never before has a powerful economy been shut down in a matter of weeks. The economy is not like a light switch that can be turned off and flipped right back on again. We have lost our confidence in a predictable economic future.

The crisis brought to the fore the divisions within our country. Our states announced that only essential businesses were to remain open. These decisions, we were told, were based on science. So if you lived in Illinois as I do, "science" decreed that liquor and marijuana stores were "essential" but clothing stores were not. "Science" decreed that elective surgery (even serious operations) were to be postponed, but abortion clinics were "essential" and could remain open.

The United States Congress directed the Federal Reserve to create trillions of dollars; and this was done by *fiat*, that is, the money was created electronically to flood the banks with liquidity.[1] Such bailouts have created a whole new sense of government dependency and entitlement. People will continue to expect free money, given that it can be created so easily.

With the loss of livelihood, and with families sheltering in place, more children were being abused. It has been projected the crisis could increase "deaths of despair," that is deaths from suicide, drug overdose, alcoholism, and the like.[2] These factors already had been killing hundreds of thousands of Americans each year, but COVID-19 threatened to compound these frightening trends.

At no other time in history has a modern industrialized economy essentially shut down, not because of a recession or mismanagement, but by government order. I'm convinced that the economic ripples will continue long after the health scare has passed. With millions unemployed and thousands of businesses reopening, it will take time, perhaps years, to rebuild. I believe several lingering effects will be a challenge for the church. How we respond will impact our future ministries both here and abroad.

As one person put it, COVID-19 is a watershed moment; not just a blizzard with a beginning and an end, but the beginning of a mini-ice age. Yes, eventually all of this might be put behind us, but the generational effects will remain. And so will the unanswered questions.

And it is not just COVID-19. While this epidemic was spreading around the world, a plague of grasshoppers had descended on East Africa. "Two new generations of locusts are set to descend on East Africa again—400 times stronger" is the headline of an April article in Quartz Africa that describes the horror of massive swarms blocking the light of the sun like a biblical plague. Hundreds of billions of these pests attacked crops in Ethiopia, Kenya, and Somalia. These ravenous creatures eat their own weight per day, destroying the food crops in these countries. No doubt thousands of people, including children, will starve as a result of this plague.[3]

Where is God in all of this?

Christians are attempting to understand this phenomenon from a God-centered point of view. Many cautioned that such things as pandemics, plagues, and natural disasters are not to be seen as something that God was orchestrating but rather just the result of a fallen world. Consequently, disease is a part of the curse. God is able to stop it, of course, but it's happening quite independently of His will and purpose. Some false prophets assured us that our suffering would be brief because they had authority over it.

This is a time when we have to think more deeply about our role as believers in a frightened and hurting world. Believing as we do in a good and sovereign God, we have to respond to questions that arise about God's relationship to the suffering of the human beings He created for His glory. And how can we help pick up the pieces of our fragmented culture?

QUESTIONS THAT NEED ANSWERS

Believers—and even non-believers—are asking a lot of questions: What is God's relationship to all of this? Did He cause these diseases and disasters, or is He just an interested observer? Is He orchestrating it? Is this a judgment from God? What kind of a God would allow such calamities to happen? Sure, we are a sinful people, but do we deserve *this*?

Also, is God obligated to deliver Christians from these disasters? If we "just trust God" as some admonish us to do, does that mean that we will get through this and come out "stronger than ever before" as they promise?

Glib answers to such questions are hurtful, not helpful. Sometimes we just need to sit beside those who grieve, letting them know we care, rather than talking to them dispassionately about God's promises and purposes. Better to say nothing than to say something that appears to trivialize the horror. There is a grief that is too deep for words, too deep for explanations, and yes, too deep for human comfort.

But yet, it's difficult for us to dismiss our questions. We want to ask whether the horrific events we have witnessed are compatible with the God who has revealed Himself in the Bible. Do not natural disasters and pandemics challenge the limits of our faith in a good and caring God? Can we watch a special report about orphaned children and keep our faith intact?

Who of us has not wondered at the seeming indifference of God toward this planet with its woes, its injustices, and its suffering? In the face of indescribable human grief, God's silence appears deafening. Or has He spoken and we've just not listened?

One observer, commenting back in 2005 on the deadly Hurricane Katrina that slammed into New Orleans, spoke for many when he said, "If this world is the product of intelligent design, then the designer has some explaining to do." Of course, many of us believe that the Designer does *not* owe us an explanation—but yet, if we believe He has revealed Himself through the Scriptures, we are permitted some insight into His ways and purposes in the world.

Only the Bible can help us answer these questions.

THE PURPOSE OF THIS BOOK

In the following pages I will discuss God's relationship to pandemics, plagues, and natural disasters. I believe that realistic answers have to be given that will ground our faith in our sovereign Lord even in a time of fear and grief—or I should say *especially* in a time of fear and grief.

Although God appears to be silent, I want to point out that He has actually spoken through the Scriptures, and furthermore, His promises are to be believed. God has entered into our world through His Word and through the Word made flesh. We have reasons to trust. We desperately need to have a fresh vision of God.

But I believe our faith must not just be the kind we often hear about from well-intentioned pastors who tell us that if we just "trust," everything will work out fine. The impression is given, if not explicitly stated, that if we trust, we will get our job back; if we trust, we will be able to make our house payments; if we trust, we will be healthy and recover from whatever ails us. I think that kind of assurance can actually do more harm than good. If things don't work out—and often they don't—we can become cynical. "So this is where trust leads us?" we say in the face of unanswered prayer . . . in the face of setbacks and continuing health and economic needs.

As we shall see later in this book, we need a hope that is not dependent on whether things work out, or whether the pain ends, or whether we see the answers to our prayers. Trust in God, yes; but trust in Him even in the face of setbacks, discouragement, and unending grief.

You will see that the apparent silence of God should not be interpreted as the indifference of God. God has not promised that we will be free from the pain of this world, but that His presence will be with us all the way to the finish line. And beyond.

My intention is not to pry into God's diary and pretend that I can see all of His purposes; indeed, there are plenty of His purposes in these disasters that will never be known to us. Ultimately, only God knows all the whys and wherefores. The older I get, the more I marvel at how mysterious God really is. Indeed, that is precisely why faith in God is so precious to Him; it is difficult to believe, but we should trust Him—we must trust Him.

Yes, I believe that God has spoken, and we must listen. Not to have all of our questions answered, but to have our faith assured. And to know that the world is not out of control.

After having read this book, if you, like Job, are encouraged to worship God despite mysteries and unanswered questions, I shall be abundantly satisfied.

A TIME TO GRIEVE

Before we delve into doctrinal waters, let us take time to simply grieve for the suffering of this present world. Let us grieve for those who have lost family members and loved ones who have succumbed to death for whatever reason. Let us grieve for the children in Kenya who will starve to death because of the locusts that have eaten their crops; let us grieve for the children left without their parents because of tornadoes and hurricanes. Let us grieve for the suffering of this planet and for the people next door who have no dependable income and face a fearful future.

Then let us turn our grief into helpfulness, doing all we can to encourage, to bless, to give money, and to risk our own selves for the sake of others. God has not left us here simply to separate ourselves from the pain around us. We are to extend ourselves to a hurting world.

If we are redeemed, we should look like our Redeemer. He wept over Jerusalem, and we should weep over the grief of this world—especially over the world's lack of genuine hope. Millions are facing death and deep suffering without any reason to believe that a day is coming when the crooked will be made straight and the suffering will have been worth the wait.

Let's take a moment to feel the pain of those who grieve.

In an article titled "Leading Beyond the Blizzard: Why Every Organization Is Now a Startup," the authors say:

Christian creativity begins with grief—the grief of a world gone wrong. It enfolds it in lament—the loud cry of Good Friday, the silence of Holy Saturday—and still comes to the tomb early Sunday morning. We are burying and saying goodbye to so much in these days, and around the world people are burying and saying goodbye to those they loved. But we do not grieve without hope. If we grieve with Jesus, and make room for others to grieve, we can hope to be visited by the Comforter, the Spirit who breathed over creation before it was even formed. And that Spirit will guide us in the choices we have to make, even on the hardest days that are ahead.[4]

John Keats wrote, "Is there another life? Shall I awake and find all this a dream? There must be, we cannot be created for this sort of suffering."[5]

And now we turn to the problem of the silence of God.

CHAPTER 2

THE SILENCE
OF GOD

God's apparent silence in the presence of human anguish is one of the greatest mysteries of our existence. When faced with gratuitous human suffering, we are forced to rethink our view of God and His relationship to the suffering on this planet. If He is omnipotent and good, why doesn't He put an end to this madness? Atheists and skeptics scoff as they ask believers hard questions about the Divine's apparent indifference to human need.

So, does God actually care about the world, or does He just *say* that He does?

Many are turning away from God in anger as they face the reality of unanswered prayer, grinding poverty, and the intensified and widespread suffering on this planet. Others are clinging to their faith in God even though they see no special reason to believe He is on their side when faced with a catastrophe.

A pandemic—just like any other disaster—can either strengthen our faith or destroy it; it can either make us seek God or turn away in disgust.

BELIEVERS HAVE BEEN HERE BEFORE

If you have a loved one who died as a result of COVID-19, or if you permanently lost your job and you don't know where your next meal is coming from, it's little comfort to be told that pandemics, plagues, and natural disasters have been happening with regularity since the beginning of human history. And yet we can't help but be encouraged by those who have gone before us. They faced the same fears and questions we do, and many of them witnessed to their faith until the very end.

Plagues and disasters of various kinds have bedeviled this world ever since the debacle in the garden of Eden, when Adam and Eve's disobedience let sin enter the world. Just type "plagues" into any search engine, and you'll find some of the major ones: the Black Death, smallpox, and the Spanish flu, in countries from ancient Babylon to modern-day America . . . the list is long. And the same is happening in many countries today amid food shortages, endless wars, and displaced peoples. The world has always been hurting, in some place more than others, but pain and loss have been the legacy of humankind.

Many Christians have often displayed unusual courage in the midst of a widespread pandemic. When plagues swept through the Roman Empire and 20 percent of the population died, the pagans took note of how the Christians suffered with hope. The pagans said with incredulity, "They carry their dead as if in triumph!"

When Marcus Aurelius spoke of caravans of wagons filled with bodies making their way through the streets of Roman cities, it was the Christians who distinguished themselves from the world around them. Indeed, some historians believe that Christianity might not have become the dominant religion of Rome were it not for these massive epidemics that gave believers the opportunity to prove the triumph of the Christian faith.

Consider: If you were a pagan and a plague swept through your city killing a third of the population, you would be terrified by such dark horrors. When your relatives died and their bodies burned, with only your own fears to guide you, you could only vainly hope that you might see them again; but you would not have the slightest assurance that you would be reunited. Nothing but terror. Unending sorrow. Hopelessness.

But Christians accepted these tragedies with hopefulness. William McNeill writes of the Christians:

> Even a shattered remnant of survivors who had somehow made it through war or pestilence or both could find warm, immediate healing and consolation in the vision of a heavenly existence for those missing relatives and friends. . . . Christianity was, therefore, a system of thought and feeling thoroughly adapted to a time of troubles in which hardship, disease, and violent death commonly prevailed.[1]

A system of thought and feeling thoroughly adapted to a time of troubles! Not only did the Christians accept the death of their friends with a note of triumph, but they were willing to risk their own lives to help others. Cyprian, Bishop of Carthage, seems almost to have welcomed the great epidemic of his time. Writing in AD 251, he claimed that only non-Christians had to fear the plague:

> How suitable, how necessary it is that this plague and pestilence, which seems horrible and deadly, searches out the justice of each and every one and examines the minds of the human race; whether the well care for the sick, whether relatives dutifully love their kinsmen as they should, whether masters show compassion for their ailing slaves, whether physicians do not desert the afflicted . . . . Although this mortality has contributed nothing else, it has especially accomplished this for Christians and servants of God, that we have begun gladly to seek martyrdom while we are learning not to fear death.

How should believers respond to those who have died? Cyprian continues:

> Our brethren who have been freed from the world by the summons of the Lord should not be mourned, since we know that they are not lost but sent before; that in departing they lead the way; that as travellers,

as voyagers are wont to be, they should be longed
for, not lamented . . . and that no occasion should be
given to pagans to censure us deservedly and justly,
on the ground that we grieve for those who we say
are living.[2]

Why grieve for those who were in the presence of
Christ? Earth was transitory; heaven was a reality. They
thought of how fortunate it was for their relatives and
friends to go before them into heaven where Christ was
waiting for them. With the apostle Paul they could say,
"To live is Christ, and to die is gain" (Philippians 1:21).
Such was the confident witness of the early Christians
that multitudes of pagans embraced the Christian faith.

Martin Luther, when confronted with the question of
whether Christians should help the sick and dying when
the plague came to Wittenberg in 1537, said that each
individual would have to answer the question for himself. He believed that the epidemic was spread by evil
spirits, but "Nevertheless, this is God's decree and punishment to which we must patiently submit and serve
our neighbor, risking our lives in this manner as St. John
teaches, 'If Christ laid down his life for us, we ought

to lay down our lives for the brethren' (1 John 3:16)."[3]
Again he writes:

> If it be God's will that evil come upon us and destroy
> us, none of our precautions will help us. Everybody
> must take this to heart: first of all, if he feels bound to
> remain where death rages in order to serve his neigh-
> bor, let him commend himself to God and say, "Lord,
> I am in thy hands; thou hast kept me here; thy will
> be done. I am thy lowly creature. Thou canst kill me
> or preserve me in the pestilence in the same way as if
> I were in fire, water, drought or any other danger."[4]

He and his wife, Katie, took sick friends into their
own home and cared for them. Yes, the plague may have
been "God's decree," but yes, we must do what we can to
save the lives of the sick and minister to the dying. And
if one dies while helping others, let the will of God be
done. Tragedies of all kinds give us the opportunity of
serving the living and the dying. Luther would tell us that
through the tragedies of others, we have the opportunity
to be pried away from our comfortable lifestyles and enter
the suffering of the world.

Jesus did not stay in heaven but entered this hurting world. He came to die a cruel death that we might be redeemed. Rather than isolating Himself from human suffering, He voluntarily "suffered . . . the righteous for the unrighteous, that he might bring us to God" (1 Peter 3:18). Early Christians believed that they should be willing to sacrifice themselves for others just as their Savior did.

The Bible presents both the reality of human suffering and death along with hope for a better future. Later in this book, I will explain the basis for such hope.

A EUROPE DIVIDED

Disasters either inspire faith or destroy it.

The Lisbon earthquake of November 1, 1755, was probably the most consequential and best known natural disaster in modern history until the Indian Ocean earthquake and tsunami that occurred late in 2004. Other disasters might have been worse, but none was so widely discussed and had such profound ramifications as what happened in Portugal. This disturbance in the physical world caused a disturbance in the spiritual world also.

That morning the sky was bright, calm, and beautiful,

but in a moment, everything was transformed into frightening chaos. The irony was that the earthquake happened on All Saints' Day when the churches were crowded with worshippers. One would think that the people who sought shelter in the houses of God might be spared. Indeed, some people ran into the churches, joining the priests who were conducting mass at 9:30 in the morning.

Eyewitnesses say the crowds had the terror of death on their faces, and when the second great shock came, priests and parishioners alike were shrieking, calling out to God for mercy, but heaven was silent to their pleas. Almost all of the churches were in rubble, and the people in them were killed. In all 30,000–40,000 died out of Lisbon's approximately 200,000 people.

As might be expected, many people clung to their faith, and others now sought out the faith, having been frightfully reminded that their lives were ever in jeopardy. People sought for meaning amid the rubble of destroyed homes and cartloads of dead bodies.

Not surprisingly, many believed this earthquake was an act of judgment against a sinful seaport city. A famous Jesuit spoke for many, "Learn, O Lisbon, that the destroyers of our houses, palaces, churches, and convents, the cause of the death of so many people and of the flames that devoured such vast treasures, are your abominable sins."[5] After all, the quake came on All Saints' Day, therefore many thought that God was saying that the sins of the saints were so grievous that they merited immediate judgment. What puzzled some, however, is that a street with brothels was largely left intact.

Predictably, Protestants were inclined to say that the earthquake was a judgment against the Jesuits who founded the city. After all, the Inquisition was in full bloom, and tens of thousands of so-called heretics had been brutally murdered. The Jesuits responded by saying that the quake revealed the anger of God because the Inquisition had become too lax.

So, whether Catholic or Protestant, there was a general consensus that this tragedy had to be interpreted in light of a transcendent world; God was somehow trying to communicate to Europe that there is a world beyond this one that can give meaning to the unpredictable and grieving world of today. Sermons on the earthquake were preached for years to come.

But the Lisbon earthquake also spawned atheism. Voltaire wrote sarcastically about those who believed in God, saying faith in God was silly and naïve. Why believe in a deity who can't even protect His people while they're worshipping in their church buildings? Better to not believe than to be betrayed by a God of power who says He cares but does nothing.

When the geologists of the day speculated that an earthquake was caused by a shift beneath the earth's crust, critics believed there was no reason to appeal to a divine being in ordering the world; earthquakes had a naturalistic explanation. The silence of a God who watched the terrified populace and did nothing to intervene was enough reason to disbelieve in the teachings of the Bible and the church.

Some historians believe that the Lisbon earthquake was the impetus that made Europe the secular continent it is today. Who needs a God who is so calloused that He would not use His power to help the terrified people worshipping Him? If there was a God, they reasoned, He was tone deaf when His help was most sorely needed.

COVID-19

People have reacted in the same way to COVID-19. On the one hand, it has sparked an interest in topics such as prayer and repentance. "Virtual" prayer meetings have sprung up everywhere. On the other hand, the secularists have seen no reason to believe in God since believers suffer the same fate as unbelievers.

Self-appointed "prophets" have risen up to tell us exactly what God is trying to tell us, and what heaven has in mind. One decreed that the "coronavirus will cease worldwide," and she declared it to be "illegal."[6] Another false prophet with a church of 15,000 members and over 1.6 million YouTube subscribers made two major predictions. First on February 29, he said that "rain would wipe away the epidemic coronavirus."[7] Then on March 1, he predicted that COVID-19 would be over on March 27, 2020.[8] On February 28, another made a similar claim: "Within a short amount of time the extreme threat will feel like it is in the way past."[9] The next day, the first American died of the virus.

But we can't talk ourselves out of a crisis.

We know of course, that we do not have the authority to declare the virus "illegal" any more than we have the authority to declare death "illegal." In the past, biblically grounded Christians prayed that the plagues would end, but they knew their future was in God's hands and not in their own.

These early Christians *did not interpret the silence of God as the indifference of God*.

Believers insisted that God was not silent: God acted when Jesus was sent to redeem us from eternal suffering, and we await a future redemption when at last even nature will be redeemed. Something is out of joint, and it awaits God to make it right. We are living on a once perfect, but now terribly flawed, planet. God has not promised deliverance from the evils of this world, but redemption for the world to come.

For Christians, COVID-19 was not an ultimate disaster. Even death itself was not a great disaster. Even death from starvation is not the ultimate disaster as we shall see later. As Paul wrote, "Our Lord Jesus Christ . . . died for us so that whether we are awake [live] or asleep [die] we might live with him" (1 Thessalonians 5:9–10). Live or die, we win.

A WINDSTORM, RAIN, AND A COLLAPSED HOUSE

Crisis reveals character.

Pandemics, plagues and natural disasters force us to make a decision. Do we trust God, or do we walk away disgusted, if not angry, with God? Natural disasters have a way of dividing humanity, getting to the bottom of our values and character. They have a way of revealing our secret loves and personal convictions—and whether we will continue to believe in the goodness of God.

Jesus told a story about a natural disaster that came to a region, exposing the inner lives of two neighbors.

Everyone then who hears these words of mine and does them will be like a wise man who built his house on the rock. And the rain fell, and the floods came, and the winds blew and beat on that house, but it did not fall, because it had been founded on the rock. And everyone who hears these words of mine and does not do them will be like a foolish man who built his house on the sand. And the rain fell, and the floods came, and the winds blew and beat against that house, and it fell, and great was the fall of it. (Matthew 7:24–27)

Consider that on a beautiful sunny afternoon, these two houses looked identical; only the powerful wind distinguished between the two. Disasters clarify our values, they challenge our faith, and they reveal who we really are. If we are rooted in the promises of Jesus, we can endure; if not, we will be swept away by our own human philosophies and narrow interpretations.

For those who find themselves distantly related to God—God as an idea, God as a construct, as our last resort in difficulty—diseases and natural disasters are only another reason to disbelieve Him and His care. But for those who have tested God by His Word and His promises, their faith will survive the onslaughts of the past and those yet to come. Will we build on sand or on the Rock?

If natural disasters do not serve God's good ends, then we are either confronted with a God who is too weak to make evil serve higher ends, or too evil to do what is good and just. Yes, there is a great danger in claiming to know too much about the whys and wherefores of God's purpose. But there is also a danger of being silent, of not saying what the Bible would allow us to say about these horrific events. I believe that pandemics and natural disasters do have an important message that we dare not ignore.

Even in God's apparent silence, He cares and can be believed.
As already emphasized, God is not silent. He has

spoken in His Word, and He has not stuttered. What follows in this book are five chapters that affirm what I believe God is saying to us as we confront the pandemics, plagues, and natural disasters of this world.

The last two chapters are our response to what the Almighty has to say. I claim no private revelations from God here, just the Bible in one hand and a hurting world in another.

Let's let God speak.

CHAPTER 3

GOD SAYS, "I AM IN CHARGE, TRUST ME."

I'm told that after an earthquake in California, a group of ministers met for a prayer breakfast. As they discussed the shifting expressways and ruined buildings, they agreed that for all practical purposes, God had nothing to do with this disaster. The earth is fallen, so earthquakes just happen according to certain laws of the natural order. Yet, surprisingly, when one of the ministers closed in prayer, he *thanked God* for the timing of the earthquake that came at 5 o'clock in the morning when there were few cars on the expressways and the sidewalks were largely empty. When he finished the prayer, his colleagues chimed in with a hearty, "Amen."

So, did God have anything to do with that earthquake or didn't He? Why should anyone thank God for the timing of the earthquake if He was but an "interested observer"? Or why should we ever pray that we would be delivered out of such a calmity if God is not directly connected to what is happening in this fallen world?

Intuitively, Chrisitans know God is in charge.

Yet, think of what this means: statistics, in themselves, are quite meaningless. Think of the two-year-old child ripped from his father's hands, thrown dozens of feet into the air, then slammed against the ground. Or, the father who crawled into a tornado shelter only to drown when it filled with water. Many such stories come to us from "tornado alley" in our southern states.

Think of the tsunami in Southeast Asia in 2004 and the terrible suffering it inflicted on an unsuspecting populace. But I've not read a more gripping account of the agony survivors endured than this account of an earthquake in Turkey several years ago. Read this and feel the anguish:

The choice is between two types of Hell—the one where you lie in sodden blankets in a muddy field or forest floor in the rain, or the one where you find any shelter on the pavements of the cities and sleep among the ruins where the rats are flourishing and the dead still lie in their thousands.

The lost people of this devastated 200-mile, industrialised corridor of north-western Turkey have made their choice. They are going into the hills in increasing numbers. Terrified and traumatised to the point where they can barely feel any grief for those who have died, they have only one thought—to get away from these obscene places they once called home.

As each hour passes, what were once bustling towns are being emptied as more than 250,000 people accept that life there is no longer possible. So great is the damage that four major towns . . . have to be razed. Not a single house in a chain of communities stretching from Istanbul to Adapazari is safe to occupy.[1]

Before we discuss God's role in these tragedies, we should pause and mourn for the horrendous pain people experience on this planet. Like the weeping prophet Jeremiah, we should say, "Arise, cry out in the night, at the beginning of the night watches! Pour out your heart like water before the presence of the Lord! Lift your hands to him for the lives of your children, who faint for hunger at the head of every street" (Lamentations 2:19).

WHAT IS GOD'S ROLE IN NATURAL DISASTERS?

Should we actually *tell* people God is in charge?

Because natural disasters in and of themselves appear to reflect very unfavorably on God, it is quite understandable that many people—I'm even speaking about Christians—want to absolve Him of any and all responsibility for these horrific events. Clearly put, they want to "get Him off the hook" in order to maintain His more loving image. In the interest of protecting His reputation, there have been many attempts to put as much distance as possible between God and nature; some speak of God as the "caring bystander," others actually affirm that God is weak and can do little about our calamities; He is a God who will eventually win, but for now He is bested by the devil.

God Is Doing the Best He Can

Let's begin with those who have opted for a weak God who is apparently unable to prevent our planet from getting pounded by one calamity after another. Tony Campolo fears that if we say God either has responsibility for natural disasters or that He does this because of a higher purpose, we will drive people away from the Christian faith. So he says that since God is not the author of evil (James 1:13), we would do well to listen to the likes of Rabbi Harold Kushner who contends that God is not as powerful as we have claimed. Campolo agrees and says that God is mighty but not omnipotent. Thus, we have "a cosmic struggle goint on between the forces of darkness and the forces of light." The good news is, that, in the end, God will win; but for now, Campolo says, "when the floods swept into the Gulf Coast, God was the first one who wept."[2]

Such stances remind me of the teachings of William James, the famous American educator, who purported that evil existed because God could not overcome it—but perhaps with our help, eventually it will be overcome, and light will cause the darkness to vanish. Unfortunately, James, humanist that he was, could not give us the assurance that God will win since it appears that the conflicting powers are rather evenly matched.

Just so, the "God" who is not omnipotent and who must deal with Hurricane Katrina as best He can after the fact, the God who weeps, but needs time to act—how can this God be trusted? We are assured that He will win in the end. But how can we be sure? If God is helpless in the face of a hurricane, how confident can we be that He will subdue all the forces of nature and the devil in the end? To believe that God is finite might get Him off the hook for natural disasters, but it also puts end-time victories in jeopardy. If the best He can do is weep for us, we're inclined to weep with Him, and perhaps even *for* Him.

The Devil Did It

There is a second way that some try to exempt God from direct involvement in natural disasters. The devil is to blame for calamities. God is not responsible for what happens. He created the world and lets it run according to certain laws; nature is fallen, and Satan, who is the god of this world, wreaks havoc with the natural order.

We should all agree that nature is indeed fallen: "Cursed is the ground because of you; in pain you shall eat of it all the days of your life; thorns and thistles it shall bring forth for you; and you shall eat the plants of the field" (Genesis 3:17–18). Somewhere I heard a story about a man who spent a great deal of his time beautifying the landscape and tending a flower garden. A friend stopped by, admired the site and said, "My, what a wonderful garden God created here!" To which the gardener replied, "Well, yes, but you should have seen what it looked like when God had it by Himself!" Yes, if we want beauty and symmetry on this cursed earth, we must tend the garden.

We are standing on scriptural ground when we say that nature is fallen and thus Satan might indeed be involved in natural disasters. We have an example of this in the book of Job when God gave Satan the power to destroy Job's children. Acting under God's direction and prescribed limitations, Satan created two natural disasters: lightning to kill the sheep and the servants and a windstorm to kill Job's ten children. Here is proof, if proof is needed, that satanic powers might indeed be connected to the natural disasters that inflict our planet.

That said, what conclusion should we draw from this? Does this mean that God is removed from nature? Does He really have a "hands-off policy" when it comes to these tragedies? Does this absolve God of all responsibility? Clearly the answer to these questions is *no*.

We must think carefully at this point. We must distinguish between the *secondary* cause of these events and their *ultimate* cause. The immediate cause of the lightning and the wind that killed Job's children was the power of Satan —but follow carefully: it was God who gave Satan the power to wreak the havoc, and it was God who prescribed the limits of what Satan could or could not do. That's why Job, quite rightly, did *not* say, "The Lord gave but the *devil* took away." No, he ascribed the death of his children to God's will. "The *Lord* gave, and the *Lord* has taken away; blessed be the name of the Lord" (Job 1:21b).

From a natural point of view, the immediate cause of the COVID-19 pandemic is that the germs which originated in Wuhan, China, spread from one person to another. The immediate cause of a tornado or hurricane is wind and temperature patterns; earthquakes take place because there are shifts beneath the earth's crust. Yet, the ultimate cause of these events is God. He rules nature either directly or through secondary causes, but either way, He is in charge. After all, He is the Creator and the sustainer of all things. We sing with Isaac Watts:

> There's not a plant or flower below
> but makes your glories known,
> and clouds arise and tempests blow
> by order from your throne.[3]

God has not relegated calamities to His hapless archrival, the devil, without maintaining strict supervision and ultimate control of nature. No earthquake comes, no tornado rages, and no tsunami washes villages away but that God signs off on it. No pandemic stalks the earth but that God allows it.

Many theologians emphasize that God does not *ordain* natural disasters and pandemics but only *permits* them to happen. However, keep in mind that the God who permits these things to happen could choose to *not* permit them to happen. In the very act of allowing them, He demonstrates that they fall within the boundaries of His inscrutable providence and will. Luther is quoted as saying, "Even the devil is God's devil."

When the disciples were at wits' end, expecting to drown, Christ awoke from His nap and said, "Peace! Be still!" The effect was immediate, "And the wind ceased, and there was a great calm" (Mark 4:39). The same Christ could have spoken similar words, and the plague of locusts in East Africa would disappear; and the rain that triggered the Venezuelan mudslides in 1999 would have been prevented. At the word of Christ, the tsunami in Southeast Asia would have ended before it began. And by His Word, the COVID-19 virus could have killed no one.

As we shall see, this gives us powerful reassurance that we are in God's hands.

THE CLEAR TEACHING OF SCRIPTURE

Let's just let the Bible speak for itself.

Who sent the flood during the time of Noah? God said, "I will bring a flood of waters upon the earth to destroy all flesh in which is the breath of life under heaven. Everything that is on the earth shall die" (Genesis 6:17). God determined the timing, the duration, and the intensity of the rain. And it happened according to His Word.

Who sent the plagues of Egypt, the hail and darkness that could be felt (Exodus 9:22; 10:21)? Who caused the sun to "stand still" so that Joshua could win a war (Joshua 10:12–15)? Who sealed the heavens during the time of Elijah and then brought rain in response to his prayer (1 Kings 18:41–46)? Who sent the earthquake that swallowed the sons of Korah who rebelled against Moses (Numbers 16:31–33)? Can anyone doubt that God is the ultimate cause of these disasters?

The biblical writer leaves no doubt as to who caused the storm that forced the sailors to throw Jonah overboard, "But the LORD hurled a great wind upon the sea, and there was a mighty tempest on the sea, so that the ship threatened to break up" (Jonah 1:4). The sailors agonized about unloading their unwanted cargo, but we read, "So they picked up Jonah and hurled him into the sea, and the sea ceased from its raging" (v. 15). It appears that the Bible is not as concerned as some theologians about God's reputation. It puts God clearly in charge of the wind, the rain, and the calamities of Earth.

In the Old Testament these were, for the most part, acts of judgment; they were God's response to disobedience. As such, these judgments generally separated the righteous from the wicked (this is not the case today, as we shall see in the next chapter). However, even back then, sometimes the righteous were victims of these judgments too. Job's children were killed, not because they were wicked, but because God wanted to test the faith of their father and mother.

On the other hand, we should note that in both the Old and New Testaments, God sent an earthquake to *help* His people. When Jonathan, the son of Saul, was out on his own battling the enemy, he killed a Philistine, and we read, "Then panic struck the whole army—those in the camp and field, and those in the outposts and raiding parties—*and the ground shook. It was a panic sent by God*" (1 Samuel 14:15 NIV).

And in the New Testament, an earthquake delivered Paul and Silas from prison. "About midnight Paul and Silas were praying and singing hymns to God, and the prisoners were listening to them, and suddenly there was a great earthquake, so that the foundations of the prison were shaken. And immediately all the doors were opened, and everyone's bonds were unfastened" (Acts 16:25–26). *Earthquakes bear the signature of God.*

But if there is still some doubt in your mind that God ultimately has control of nature, let me ask: Have you ever prayed for beautiful weather for a wedding? Have you ever prayed for rain at a time of drought? Have you ever prayed for protection during a lightning storm?

Many people who do not believe that God controls the weather change their minds when a funnel cloud comes toward them.

The ministers in San Francisco were right in giving God thanks that the earthquake came early in the morning when there was little traffic on the expressways. They were wrong, however, for saying that God was not ultimately responsible for the tragedy. Of course He was—both biblically and logically, it can be no other way.

THE BLESSING OF GOD'S SOVEREIGNTY

I personally can accept tragedies much better if I know that they have come from God's hands than I can if I am the victim of uncontrolled random forces of nature. *If COVID-19 is out of God's hands, then I am out of God's hands. After all, I could die of the virus.*

As John Calvin, who had many physical ailments, is reported to have said, "I am greatly afflicted but it is from thy hand, therefore I am abundantly satisfied." It is easier for me to trust in God if I know that He is personally in charge than if He's only an interested bystander. John Piper said it outright, "The coronavirus was sent, therefore, by

God. This is not a season for sentimental views of God. It is a bitter season. And God ordained it. God governs it. He will end it. No part of it is outside his sway. Life and death are in his hand."[4]

Yes, of course, I know that we as humans are also responsible for the way we live and how we care for (or *don't* care for) our bodies. So, we eat as healthy as possible, we attempt to exercise, and during a pandemic, we follow all of the guidelines our health experts give us. Along with His providential care, God keeps us alive by giving us the wisdom to do the best we can to stay alive as long as possible.

These disasters are also used by God to test our faith and to give us the opportunity to become involved in the pain around us. As a church, we are called to be a beacon of light and a help to a very hurting world. Jesus wept at the tomb of Lazarus, and we must weep and act sacrificially to bring healing and comfort to those who mourn. Most of all, we must introduce the world to the good news of the gospel, which saves us from even greater future calamities. More on that later.

The compatibility between God's sovereignty and human responsibility is a doctrinal matter well beyond the scope of this chapter. But we must believe that we have a responsibility to care for ourselves and others on this planet, and yet also believe that we die within God's providential timing and will. Jesus assured His children that they were secure within the details of His providential care. "Are not five sparrows sold for two pennies? And not one of them is forgotten before God. Why, even the hairs of your head are all numbered. Fear not; you are of more value than many sparrows" (Luke 12:6–7). The God who cares for the lilies of the field and the sparrows that fall is ultimately in charge of nature. And in charge of us.

His sovereignty covers all aspects of nature. "Whatever the LORD pleases, he does, in heaven and on earth, in the seas and all deeps. He it is who makes the clouds rise at the end of the earth, who makes lightnings for the rain and brings forth the wind from his storehouses" (Psalm 135:6–7). If you don't believe that nature is under God's control, He does not deserve your worship.

Trust Him we must.

SHOULD WE BLESS GOD OR CURSE HIM?

So, is God to be blamed? That word *blame* implies wrongdoing; therefore, such a word should never be applied to the Almighty. Even saying that God is responsible for natural disasters might not be best since the word *responsibility* usually implies accountability. God, however, is accountable to no one. "Our God is in the heavens; he does all that he pleases" (Psalm 115:3). It is best, I believe, simply to say that God is in charge of what happens on His planet, either directly or indirectly through secondary causes.

Job faced a sorrowful dilemma: he clearly understood that God used natural disasters to take his children, and yet to his everlasting credit, he didn't blame God but "fell on the ground and worshiped" (1:20). But later when he found himself sitting on an ash heap with his body covered with boils, his wife, trying to manage his inconsolable grief suggested, "Curse God and die" (2:9).

Interestingly, some translations quote her as saying "*Bless* God and die." The reason is because the Hebrew word *barakh* actually means *bless*, only the context determines the meaning. The preponderance of scholars believe that she used this word as a euphemism for *curse*; to say "curse God" was too great a blasphemy. What is more, she did not realize that she was actually echoing the very words Satan told God that Job would say if he lost his family or his health (see 1:11; 2:5). Job's strong response to her as "a foolish woman" makes it clear that what she really meant was "*Curse* God and die."

But Job would have none of it. Instead, he answered, "Shall we receive good from God, and shall we not receive evil?" (2:10). Twice we read, "In all this Job did not sin or charge God with wrong" (1:22; see also 2:10). He chose to *bless* rather than *curse*.

Today we know that many people curse God when tragedy strikes; perhaps they don't use the word, but they turn away from Him in anger and disgust. They find it intolerable to believe that God could have some wise purpose in all their suffering. But we must believe that God has a good and all-wise purpose for the heartrending that disasters bring.

Speaking of the earthquake in Turkey that took thousands of lives, John Piper says that God had "hundreds of thousands of purposes, most of which will remain hidden to us until we are able to grasp them at the end of the age."[5] God has a purpose for each individual, whether dead or alive.

As finite beings, we cannot judge an infinite being. God is not obligated to tell us all that He's up to. As Paul reminded an imaginary objector to God's sovereignty, the clay has no right to judge the potter. It is not necessary for us to know God's purposes in order to believe that such purposes do exist. This is the kind of faith that delights His heart. "And without faith it is impossible to please him" (Hebrews 11:6a).

Job's choice is ours. When tragedy comes into our lives, we can bless God or curse Him. Some have chosen to curse, others have made the wiser choice . . . to bless God. Later in this book I will share what I say to those who choose to curse rather than bless.

What follows is a modern-day Job story about a couple who chose to bless God and not curse Him. A couple, who like Job and his wife, were faced with dead children and plenty of unanswered questions. But they understood that in the midst of untold grief, God was still their refuge and strength.

A MODERN-DAY JOB STORY

On November 8, 1994, Pastor Scott Willis and his wife Janet were traveling with six of their nine children on I-94 near Milwaukee when a piece of metal fell off the truck ahead of them. Scott had no choice but to let the object pass under his vehicle. The rear gas tank exploded, resulting in five of the six children dying in the flames. The sixth child, Benjamin, was helicoptered to a hospital but died the next day.

Scott and Janet were able to get out of the vehicle, sustaining burns from which they would later recover. Standing there watching their children die in the fire, Scott said to Janet, "They are with the Lord; God has prepared us for this." He encouraged her to quote the Psalm they had been memorizing, "I will bless the LORD at all times; his praise shall continually be in my mouth" (Psalm 34:1). Don't miss it: they *blessed* at the time when their precious children were being taken from them.

The loss they sustained is beyond description. They knew they could not grieve for six children all at the same time. So, they agreed that on Sunday they would grieve for the oldest of the children killed; Monday they would grieve for the next oldest and so on. Christ walked with them through the deep sorrows of this tragedy despite nights of weeping, depression, and unanswered questions.

Scott and Janet have become dear friends of ours, and knowing them up close and personal, we have caught a small glimpse of their long and painful journey. Even now, more than twenty-five years later, they explain, "Every morning we awake we say, this is one more day to prove the faithfulness of God. Every night we say, we are one day closer to seeing our children again." Janet says she lives with the confidence that their children are safe and well taken care of.

Such is the testimony of this couple who understood that children are a gift of God; and when God wants them back, He has the right to take them to Himself. Job, the Old Testament patriarch, would agree.

We say that the Willis family had an accident, but they also see this tragedy as part of God's providential plan. What we call an accident might be a well-planned event from God's point of view.

Just think of the contingencies, the events that had to come together for this accident to happen. Here are a few: *If only* they had started their trip a minute earlier in the morning (or a minute later). Then again, *if only* the truck had been at a different location on the expressway; either a few seconds earlier or later. Or, *if only* that piece of metal had fallen earlier or later; or if it had scuttled into the ditch rather than in the middle of the lane of traffic.

We can identify a dozen "if onlys." After all, this accident would not have happened unless a number of circumstances had converged at the precise time and the exact place.

Scott and Janet would tell us to take those "if onlys" and draw a circle around them. Then label the circle, "the providence of God." The Christian believes that God is greater than our "if onlys." His providential hand encompasses the whole of our lives, not just the good days but the "bad" days too. We have the word *accident* in our vocabulary; God does not. For God there are no random events.

Accidents, ill health, being murdered, dying in a natural disaster—God uses all of these means to bring His children home. We often can't control events outside of us; we are, however, responsible for how we react to what happens in the seemingly random events of life. God can send any chariot He wishes to fetch us for Himself.

William Cowper, who struggled with depression and even attempted suicide, put the mysteries of God in perspective:

> GOD moves in a mysterious way,
>   His wonders to perform;

He plants his footsteps in the sea,
And rides upon the storm.

Deep in unfathomable mines
Of never-failing skill;
He treasures up his bright designs,
And works his sovereign will.

Ye fearful saints fresh courage take,
The clouds ye so much dread
Are big with mercy, and shall break
In blessings on your head.

Judge not the LORD by feeble sense,
But trust him for his grace;
Behind a frowning providence,
He hides a smiling face.

His purposes will ripen fast,
Unfolding ev'ry hour;
The bud may have a bitter taste,
But sweet will be the flow'r.

> Blind unbelief is sure to err,
> And scan his work in vain;
> GOD is his own interpreter,
> And he will make it plain.[6]

"Grieve not because thou understands not life's mystery," wrote a wise man, "Behind the veil is concealed many a delight."[7] The trusting believer knows this is so.

"The LORD gave, and the LORD has taken away; blessed be the name of the LORD" (Job 1:21).

CHAPTER 4

GOD SAYS, "THERE ARE LESSONS YOU SHOULD LEARN."

Obviously, we are to learn from nature.

God wants us to look at the heavens and see His glory (see Psalm 19:1–6). Jesus encouraged His disciples to look at the lilies of the field and the birds of the air to see examples of God's faithfulness (Matthew 6:25–30). When we see a sparrow fall to the ground it should remind us that God does care for sparrows despite their oft-untimely deaths. But we are also to learn from the terror which nature can inflict on us.

I must emphasize that when I speak about "lessons to

be learned" from pandemics and natural disasters, I do not mean to imply that I'm giving *reasons* as to why God sends these devastations to the world. Ultimately, the real reasons are known only to Him, and He has not seen fit to reveal the details. Nor do I wish to imply that these lessons will bring immediate comfort to those who suffer in loneliness and pain. Let us candidly admit that *even if we knew all the reasons why God sent a disease or disaster, it would not completely remove the pain of loss and grief.*

Jesus shed some light on the question of human tragedy when He referred to a collapsed tower under which eighteen men were buried.

LESSONS FROM A TOPPLED TOWER

When Jesus was told about a group of Galileans butchered by Pilate, who mixed their blood with their animal sacrifices, He answered, "Do you think that these Galileans were worse sinners than all the other Galileans, because they suffered in this way? No, I tell you; but unless you repent, you will all likewise perish" (Luke 13:2–3). Of course, we are not surprised that the martyrs were not greater sinners than others, since martyrdom is often a credit to one's faith; indeed, Jesus Himself was brutally murdered.

But then He continues, "Or those eighteen on whom the tower in Siloam fell and killed them: do you think that they were worse offenders than all the others who lived in Jerusalem? No, I tell you; but unless you repent, you will all likewise perish" (vv. 4–5). Here was a tragedy known and talked about in the city of Jerusalem. It's quite possible that this tower was an aqueduct built by Romans who were employing Jews in its construction. The Jewish Zealots would have, of course, disapproved of Jewish workers helping with a project that would benefit their despised oppressors. We can hear it already, "Those men deserved to die . . . they were victims of God's judgment!" The self-righteous pointed fingers in those days too! Jesus, however, gave a different interpretation of the event.

I realize that a fallen tower is not what we call a natural disaster; almost certainly this happened because it was poorly constructed. But Jesus used this incident to point out that disasters do not separate the wicked from the righteous. Those who died when the tower collapsed were not greater sinners than others in Jerusalem. It was both morally wrong and self-righteous to sit in judgment of those who were killed so unexpectedly.

From God's standpoint, disasters might be meticulously planned, but from our perspective, they occur haphazardly, randomly. We have no right to think they divide the human race into two separate categories of righteous and wicked.

God's relationship with Israel was quite different. In Old Testament times, God ruled the Jewish nation directly; He dealt with them as a group that lived within a certain geographical area. Thus often (though not always) there was a direct cause-effect relationship between their obedience and the cooperation of natural forces. God said He would use nature to reward or punish the people (see 2 Chronicles 7:13–14). Locusts and plagues were sent as a judgment for disobedience; rain and good crops as a reward for obedience.

Contrast this with today when good crops are sometimes given even when a nation turns from God, such as in Western Europe and the United States. We've often observed that just as unbelievers are blessed along with believers, so the righteous are often victims along with unbelievers. Disasters appear to come blindly and without regard to positions, status, or age.

When Hurricane Katrina hit the Gulf of Mexico in 2005, some people said it was the judgment of God on the ungodly city of New Orleans. But was New Orleans any more wicked than, say, Las Vegas? What did Tuscaloosa, Alabama, do to deserve the EF4 tornado that ripped the town killing at least sixty-four and injuring 1,500 people back in 2011? Parts of the town were totally decimated by winds up to 190 miles per hour.

Let me be clear. Tragedies separate people into two camps: the dead and the living, not the saved and the damned; not the religious and irreligious. The righteous die with the wicked.

LESSONS FOR US

Why are such disasters random? In the book of Job, we have a list of weather patterns: thunder, lightning, downpours, whirlwinds, snow and ice; and then we read, "They turn around and around by his guidance, to accomplish all that he commands them on the face of the habitable world. Whether for correction for his land or for love he causes it to happen" (Job 37:12–13). The upheavals of nature bring correction for us, showing both God's judgments and His love.

What should we be learning?

The Uncertainty of Life

Unexpected calamities confirm the words of James, "Yet you do not know what tomorrow will bring. What is your life? For you are a mist that appears for a little time and then vanishes" (James 4:14). The people who lose their lives in a natural disaster did not wake that morning telling themselves, "This could be my last day on earth." Too often we think that what happened to them will not happen to us.

When you read the obituaries of those who have died in sudden calamities, you should visualize your own name in the column. When we grieve with the families, we should remind ourselves that we could die at any moment. Natural disasters and global pandemics should be reminders that death might be just around the next corner.

I read about one couple who left California for fear of earthquakes and died in a tornado in Missouri! Life is a loan from God. He gives it and He takes it. And He can take it whenever and however He wills. This sounds heartless, but C. S. Lewis was right when he pointed out that war does not increase death; all the victims of such disasters would have to die by virtue of old age.

Cruel as it sounds, death is determined for all of us, whether by cancer, an accident, a natural disaster, or COVID-19. Death is a scheduled, divine appointment. Tragedies rid us of the overconfidence we have that we are in control of our destiny.

Disasters, in the words of David Miller, remind us that "Human existence on Earth was not intended to be permanent. Rather, the Creator intended life on Earth to serve as a temporary interval of time . . . in which people are given the opportunity to attend to their spiritual condition as it relates to God's will for living. Natural disasters provide people with conclusive evidence that life on Earth is brief and uncertain."[1]

COVID-19 jerked us into reality. Even those who thought death was far off discovered that it could be as near as the ER in their local hospital.

What would we do today if we knew we would die by the weekend? We should do those things now. And, most importantly, today is the day of salvation. Tomorrow might be too late.

Our Values Are Clarified

When that tower in Siloam fell, no one mourned the loss of the bricks, but eighteen families mourned the loss of a husband, father, or brother. As Max Lucado says, when you listen to the words of survivors of Katrina, "No one laments a lost plasma television or submerged SUV. No one runs through the streets yelling, 'My cordless drill is missing' or 'My golf clubs have washed away.' If they mourn, it is for people lost. If they rejoice, it is for people found."[2] He goes on to say that raging hurricanes and broken levees have a way of prying our fingers off the stuff we love. One day you have everything; the next day you have nothing.

As a pastor, I've seen how the suffering of a child or the death of a loved one suddenly gives those who grieve a whole new set of lenses through which to view the world. Our tendency to give first-rate attention to second-rate priorities is exposed, and we awake to the realization that someday the world and everything in it will be burned up and all that will remain is angels, demons, human beings, and God.

The great French philosopher and mathematician, Blaise Pascal, was surely right when he said, "Man's sensitivity to trivia, and his insensitivity to matters of major importance, reveal he has a strange disorder."[3] It usually takes a tragedy to make us realize that people matter and things don't. It divides time and eternity, this world from the next. And to further clarify our values, Jesus also said, "For what will it profit a man if he gains the whole world and forfeits his soul?" (Matthew 16:26).

We should see COVID-19 as a wake-up call for us to invest in eternity and not the fleeting values of time. Though we are here today, we could be gone tomorrow.

Money Cannot Keep Its Promises

COVID-19 was no respecter of persons. The rich died with the poor, and the high and mighty suffered along with the lowly. The rich are better positioned to endure the pandemic, but death will overtake them as well. "One's life does not consist in the number of his possessions" (Luke 12:15).

Of course, money is important for our livelihood. And having lots of money, if used wisely and shared generously, can be a great blessing. Money is the reward for our work, and it buys food for our families, pays the rent (or mortgage), and helps our children get an education. Jesus taught that it could be invested in ways that bring eternal dividends. My point is not to disparage money but to highlight its dangers.

Money is deceptive because it makes all of the same promises as God. It says, "I will be with you in sickness and in health; I will be with you when the stock market is up and when it is down." It promises cradle to grave security and assures us that it cannot only clothe and feed us, but purchase anything we need to stave off the specter of death.

Several years ago I took an all-day guided tour of a few of the cemeteries here in Chicago. I noticed that unknown people were buried next to the rich and famous. Some grave stones were small with only a name and the dates; others were mausoleums, adorned with long tributes. Communist rioters were buried in the same cemetery as well-known nineteenth century industrialists. They all varied in age, in influence and in status. What they had in common was that they were equal in death.

Somewhere I read a story about some gold miners who were caught in a terrible winter up north; they sat with a pile of gold on their table, but eventually starved to death. They sacrificed their lives for gold, but in the end, it could not save them. Think of the many who have sacrificed their family and even their honor to get money, but their lives ended in bitter disappointment, and their money was of no help.

Mark Zuckerberg, cofounder and CEO of Facebook, believes money can eventually cure all diseases. He and his wife, Priscilla Chan, started an initiative in 2015, with the goal of wiping out all disease by the end of the century. He and his wife plan to donate 99 percent of their Facebook shares and $3 billion over the next decade to the initiative.[4] Perhaps it will work, though I have my doubts. No matter how successful Zuckerberg's money is in stemming disease, it cannot eliminate death.

With the collapse of much of our economy due to COVID-19, those who lived beyond their means found themselves with debts they couldn't pay. They disregarded the warning of James, "Come now, you who say, 'Today or tomorrow we will go into such and such a town and spend a year there and trade and make a profit'—yet you do not know what tomorrow will bring. What is your life? For you are a mist that appears for a little time and then vanishes" (James 4:13–14). Many who had confidence that their tomorrow would simply be a continuation of the past, were shocked to learn that their future was in serious jeopardy. Bankruptcies have erupted in unexpected places.

The volatility of the stock market reminded investors they could not control the fluctuation of the markets, not knowing whether to buy or sell. Suddenly the future became very unpredictable. And money itself was no guarantee that they could buy their way out of sickness and eventual death.

If you have made some unwise financial decisions, or if you lost your job and are unable to pay your bills, remember God has not abandoned you. He is available to give you the wisdom you need for your next moves. Here is a promise I have claimed many times: "If any of you lacks wisdom, let him ask God, who gives generously to all without reproach, and it will be given him. But let him ask in faith, with no doubting" (James 1:5–6). Seek wisdom, ask God. He will guide you.

I shall end this by simply quoting God's Word. "But those who desire to be rich fall into temptation, into a snare, into many senseless and harmful desires that plunge people into ruin and destruction. For the love of money is a root of all kinds of evils. It is through this craving that some have wandered away from the faith and pierced themselves with many pangs" (1 Timothy 6:9–10).

The COVID-19 pandemic has proven that money can't save us. Yes, we need money to pay our bills, but it does not offer as much security as promised. Only what Jesus called "the true riches" can greet us in the life to come.

The Danger of Self-Delusion

We are tempted, of course, to say that gruesome calamities are always bad while health and happiness are always good. But Jesus told a story that proved that such superficial evaluations can be deceptive. According to the story, a rich man who enjoyed life found himself in torment after he died; whereas, a beggar who suffered in this life found himself in bliss (see Luke 16:19–31). This sudden reversal of fortune reminds us that our judgments of today might have to be severely revised tomorrow! Enjoying life when all is going well might actually blind us to reality.

In one of his most popular books, *The Screwtape Letters,* C. S. Lewis imagines a lead demon, Screwtape, writing letters to Wormwood, a demonic underling, to give him advice on how to deceive humans. We would think that war might be a great boon to the strategy of the devil, but Screwtape says that he and the other demons should not expect too much from the war; they can hope for a good deal of cruelty and unchasteness, but if the demons are not careful they might "see thousands turning . . . to the Enemy [God], while tens of thousands who do not go so far as that will nevertheless have their attention diverted from themselves to values and causes which they believe to be higher than the self."[5] Thus, in wartime, men prepare for death in ways they do not when things are going smoothly.

Then the demon continues.

How much better for us if *all* humans died in costly nursing homes amid doctors who lie, nurses who lie, friends who lie, as we have trained them, promising life to the dying, encouraging the belief that sickness excuses every indulgence, and even, if our workers know their job, withholding all suggestions of a priest lest it should betray to the sick man his true condition![6]

Lewis believes—and I concur—that "contented worldliness" is one of the demon's best weapons at times of peace. But when disasters come, this weapon is rendered worthless. He writes, "In wartime not even a human can believe that he is going to live forever."[7]

This is one of the reasons why we will never know all of God's purposes in mass disasters—we simply do not know the thousands who turned to God when threatened with COVID-19. Spiritually careless people are forced to take God seriously in a time of crisis. Some harden their hearts but others turn to God in desperation.

The reality of imminent death has a way of focusing the mind on eternity.

A Lesson About Repentance

"Unless you repent, you shall likewise perish!"

The collapse of the tower of Siloam was a visual demonstration of what will happen to the unrepentant, except that their destruction will not be temporal, it will be eternal. And pandemics, plagues and natural disasters convey the same message.

Thankfully, God is not subject to lockdowns, social distancing, or sheltering in place. During the COVID-19 crisis, churches began to have "virtual prayer meetings" asking God for deliverance from this terrible pandemic. As long as everything was going along quite fine, prayer was optional, but suddenly when our lives were on the line, we remembered that we desperately needed God.

We should be distressed over the lack of prayerful repentance in our churches—I'm speaking about our evangelical churches—especially in America today. When I was much younger, every gospel-loving church had a prayer meeting each week, usually Wednesday evening. Today, few churches are called together for prayer, unless of course, a catastrophe strikes.

When our physical lives are threatened, we call on God; when our spiritual lives are threatened, we excuse it and move on to the next thing on our agenda. COVID-19 is God's moment to purge our souls, not just God's moment to protect our bodies. John Piper puts it vividly:

> But, oh, how we feel our physical pain! How indignant we can become if God touches our bodies! We may not grieve over the way we demean God every day in our hearts. But let the coronavirus come and threaten our bodies, and he has our attention. Or does he? *Physical pain is God's trumpet blast to tell us that something is dreadfully wrong in the world.*[8]

Should we pray? Yes. But for *what* should we pray? For physical deliverance? Yes, but more importantly, for spiritual deliverance. We need spiritual healing more than physical healing.

When the apostles were persecuted, they didn't pray for the persecution to stop, they prayed for faithfulness in persecution. Paul didn't even pray to be released from prison but rather that he'd be a good witness to the guards. Even as we pray that God would end the pandemic, our prayer should primarily be that we would be good witnesses in the midst of the pandemic rather than for deliverance from it.

Today, there is leaven in the church that must be purged. There is the acceptance of impurity, addictions to technology, pornography, and the dominance of pleasure. We have widespread apathy about witnessing to our friends about the gospel.

What right do we have to ask God to stay His hand and bring an end to our physical suffering? Why should our desire to be free of disease be more important than our desire to be cleansed by the "washing of water with the word, so that he might present the church to himself in splendor, without spot or wrinkle or any such thing, that she might be holy and without blemish" (Ephesians 5:26b–27)? Diseases of the soul are far more destructive than diseases of the body.

Let's bow in prayer right now in repentance and faith. Even as Paul shook the viper into the fire, may we separate ourselves from the sins that so easily beset us.

"Unless you repent, you will likewise perish."

CHAPTER 5

GOD SAYS, "YOU LIVE IN A WORLD THAT IS UNDER JUDGMENT."

Was COVID-19 the judgment of God? Or what about the massive 2010 earthquake in Haiti? Or the tornadoes in Georgia? The locusts in East Africa?

I will answer those questions, but first I have to point out that the word *judgment* is used in various ways in Scripture, so I will highlight some of broad categories for the sake of context. Note that there are other words such as *condemnation* that essentially have the same meaning.

ASPECTS OF BIBLICAL JUDGMENT

Adam and Eve's disobedience set in motion a number of different judgments. The aftermath of their disobedience resulted in both short-term and long-term consequences, and all of us are affected in one way or another. Let's try to unpack several effects of the fall.

The Judgment of This World

The entrance of sin into the world meant that the entire human race is under the judgment of God. Let us hear the words of Jesus who taught that only those who believe in Him are exempt from this judgment, from this condemnation, "Whoever believes in him [Jesus] is not condemned, but *whoever does not believe is condemned already*, because he has not believed in the name of the only Son of God" (John 3:18).

Before we became believers, we were "by nature children of wrath, like the rest of mankind" (Ephesians 2:3). We are born children of wrath, both by nature and later by choice, and if we don't respond to God's gracious redemption, we will remain that way forever. Again Jesus said, "Whoever believes in the Son has eternal life; whoever does not obey the Son shall not see life, but *the wrath of God remains on him*" (John 3:36).

On a practical level, this universal judgment accounts for spiritual blindness, an openness to self-deception and emptiness. Here's how Paul described it: "For we ourselves were once foolish, disobedient, led astray, slaves to various passions and pleasures, passing our days in malice and envy, hated by others and hating one another" (Titus 3:3). No sugarcoating of human nature here.

Just listen to the headlines on our news channels, and you'll agree that this is an apt description of the human race. Beneath the veneer of the best civilization there is an undercurrent of selfish and angry behavior ready to erupt when the circumstances are right. Take away what people think they deserve and just see what happens. We are not nearly as good as we think we are.

And there is more.

The Judgment of Death

Back to COVID-19. Was this a judgment from God? Yes, because death itself is a judgment, and such tragedies accelerate the process of death for thousands of people. The same can be said for famines, tornadoes, hurricanes, mudslides, and earthquakes. Not to mention cancer, heart disease, and innumerable other kinds of aliments that plague this planet.

God said to Adam and Eve, ". . . for in the day that you eat of it you shall surely die" (Genesis 2:17). They ate, and that very day they began their journey to death—and because of their disobedience, you and I are born as sinners with an expiration date. As the apostle Paul put it, "Therefore, just as sin came into the world through one man, and death through sin, and so death spread to all men because all sinned" (Romans 5:12). Death is a judgment.

Every day about 7,500 people die in the United States, and over 150,000 die worldwide. That's about 55 million deaths per year. Natural disasters only catch our attention when they are of great magnitude with many simultaneous deaths and enormous costs in property damages. They are a dramatic acceleration of what happens all the time. The process of death is just intensified during a mass disaster.

For many people in the world—for many tens of thousands—they are experiencing a devastating personal disaster every day. Every day, accidents are taking the lives of many, and scores of people are being displaced. Famines are raging, people are dying of hunger, cancer, heart disease, and, for some, it is COVID-19. Death is everywhere.

Even though Christ died for our sins, we as Christians will still die because death is a judgment that has passed on to all humankind. Jesus removed the sting of death, but physical death will come to us nonetheless. Think of it this way: the whole earth is under a curse, and we as believers are a part of that corruption. No matter how godly and Spirit-filled, we also become victims of present tragedies and judgment in this fallen world.

I've already made the point that none of the disasters mentioned in this book increase the number of people who will die. Eventually the children, youth, and adults will die; the statistics on death are sobering. As mentioned, widespread calamities highlight the fact that often people die in mass numbers rather than living to what we regard as a normal lifespan. When we hear about a disaster, we fear we will die sooner than we had hoped.

Christians are also subject to other judgments. Peter taught that Christians are judged during times of persecution. They are tested by God and disciplined; this too is a form of judgment. "For it is time for judgment to begin at the household of God; and if it begins with us, what will be the outcome for those who do not obey the gospel of God? And 'If the righteous is scarcely saved, what will become of the ungodly and the sinner?'" (1 Peter 4:17–18).

When God sends judgments to His children, it is not to punish them, but rather to discipline them. And some day we will even be in attendance at the judgment seat of Christ (2 Corinthians 5:10). At that event, we will give an account for the way we lived; either we will receive rewards or be denied them. But thankfully, we will be spared eternal judgment. In fact, Jesus made the astounding claim, "Truly, truly, I say to you, if anyone keeps my word, he will never see death" (John 8:51). Yes, we will die, but the transition will be so fleeting, we will not "see" its true horror.

Natural disasters are judgments, for the obvious reason that all physical death and destruction is a judgment of God. As emphasized, death for the believer is a judgment that is temporary; for the unbeliever, however, there awaits a conscious eternal death. Meanwhile, in this life, the prospect of our physical death shouts to all of us, reminding us that time is no match for eternity. We are warned, "And just as it is appointed for man to die once, and after that comes judgment" (Hebrews 9:27).

The Immediate Consequences of Sin Are Judgments

Often we hear statements such as, "If we don't repent, God is going to judge America!" We forget that all sin carries with it some immediate consequences. America is already under judgment, continuous judgment. In the book of Deuteronomy, God warned the Jews that if they didn't repent, they would experience a series of judgments, culminating in the destruction of their families. "Your sons and your daughters shall be given to another people, while your eyes look on and fail with longing for them all day long, but you shall be helpless" (Deuteronomy 28:32). Indeed, children and their parents will be starving, and there will be no way to save them (vv. 54–55).

The terrible effects of the destruction of the family is one of God's judgments against our nation. Our condoning of immorality, pornography, and even widespread acceptance of homosexual marriages—all of this is proof that God's hand is being removed from us as we plunge headlong into personal and national rebellion. As a result, our children are suffering from predators, from sexual abuse within their own families, and from self-absorbed, uncaring parents.

I've been asked, "Is God mad at America?" Let's let Paul answer the question: "For the wrath of God is revealed from heaven against all ungodliness and unrighteousness of men, who by their unrighteousness suppress the truth" (Romans 1:18). What follows in this passage is a description of sins—particularly homosexual acts—with the ominous statement that "God gave them up" occurring three times (vv. 24, 26, 28). No nation has sinned against the light of God's Word as we have.

God is not mad at America, but He is angry with unrepentant sinners. On the other hand, He is gracious to those who respond to His mercy as found in Jesus Christ, "Since, therefore, we have now been justified by his blood, much more shall we be saved by him from the wrath of God" (Romans 5:9). He is angry, yes, but also gracious.

COVID-19, plagues, earthquakes, tsunamis, tornadoes, famines—they are all judgments and they are all saying the same thing: we have greatly sinned both individually, as churches and as a nation. God is awakening us to our great need for repentance. Yes, He has our attention.

The Nature of the World Mirrors Our Nature

I'm sure we have all observed that we as human beings can do some incredibly good things but also some incredibly bad things. We can be compassionate, caring, and sacrificial, but we can also be vindictive, selfish, and even destructive.

Nature behaves in the same way. A beautiful, sunny day warms our bodies and lifts our spirits, but too much sun can produce a desert. The rain that blesses a crop can also turn into hail that destroys it. The wind that refreshes us can become a tornado that kills us.

Why this similarity between us and nature? When Adam and Eve disobeyed God, they came under the curse of sin; and then nature followed their lead. God put nature under a curse (Genesis 3:17–18). A fallen people were doomed to live in a fallen environment. So nature was reordered and is fallen just as we are. Both we and nature are in need of redemption.

Left to ourselves, we are filled with suspicion, greed, and fear. We will take advantage of others to enrich ourselves; we will become obsessed with self-interest, caring little for the welfare of our neighbor. John Piper writes, "We humans are finite, sinful, culturally conditioned, and shaped (and misshaped) by our genes and personal history. Out of our hearts and minds and mouths come every manner of self-justifying rationalization for our own preferences."[1] He writes that our "dishonoring of God's glory makes us worthy objects of holy wrath."[2] Even the best of people need the gift of righteousness that comes only through Jesus Christ.

Like us, nature can be terrible. And when it is, it is a visual demonstration of how horrible sin is. When we see the effects of a tornado, we should tell ourselves that this is a picture of what sin does: it brings moral and spiritual destruction to human beings, leaving them ruined and destitute. When Katrina devastated New Orleans, people were surprised at the amount of pornography that was floating in the streets. Just so, sin exposes our dark side. Physical evil is a picture of the moral evil that bedevils this world. Nature was cursed after man fell, and it can only be redeemed after we are redeemed. Nature longs for redemption but it must wait for us. We get first dibs.

Read carefully:

I consider that our present sufferings are not worth comparing with the glory that will be revealed in us.

For the creation waits in eager expectation for the children of God to be revealed. For the creation was subjected to frustration, not by its own choice, but by the will of the one who subjected it, in hope that the creation itself will be liberated from its bondage to decay and brought into the freedom and glory of the children of God. We know that the whole creation has been groaning as in the pains of childbirth right up to the present time. (Romans 8:18–22 NIV)

The Bible does not minimize the groaning of this present creation. Unlike some of the eastern religions that deny the existence of evil, Christianity speaks the truth about the reality of suffering. It does not give us false hope that things will work out well in this life. It does not guarantee that people who lost their jobs during the COVID-19 crisis will get their job back or that they will be spared from the virus. In the Bible, hope is always presented in terms of eternity, not time.

Paul begins by saying that "our present sufferings are not worth comparing with the glory that will be revealed in us." Suffering is redeemable; the future will make up for the present. The last chapter has yet to be written.

Answers that elude us in this life will become clear in the life to come.

Joni Erickson Tada, who has lived and ministered for fifty years from a wheelchair, quoted these words to me, though I cannot remember the source. "When we get to heaven, we will be surprised at how little we suffered on earth and that we suffered badly."

Don't miss Paul's bottom line: When man sinned, humankind was cursed, and the physical universe followed suit. Now Paul says the physical creation "waits in eager expectation" (the imagery is that creation waits "on tip toe") for us to be redeemed so that it can also then be redeemed and restored to its original pristine state. At the return of Christ, we will be resurrected and redeemed, and with the establishment of the new heaven and earth, the curse of sin that hangs over nature will be forever lifted.

Until then, the people of God also share in the judgment of death. And before God wraps up history, more judgments will still fall on this planet. We have not seen the end.

COVID-19 got our attention. God warns us from heaven, "Prepare to meet your God" (Amos 4:12).

And the worst is still to come.

CHAPTER 6

GOD SAYS, "THE WORST IS YET TO COME."

U nless you repent, you shall likewise perish!"
    If you've been in a theater, you know they always show previews of upcoming movies. On the few times Rebecca and I attended, the previews were so filled with violence and mayhem that I wondered who would want to see the actual movie. Be that as it may, the preview gives a hint at what is to come.

Pandemics, plagues, and natural disasters are previews of the upheavals and suffering that is to come. I just recently reread the book of Revelation to see how many of the coming judgments have already been taking place on planet Earth, many since the beginning of creation. In the future tribulation, there will be pestilence, earthquakes, famine, powerful wind, and plagues too numerous to mention.

The starry heavens reflect the glory of God; calm winds and sunshine remind us of the mercy of God; the upheavals of nature are to demonstrate the judgment of God. If the heavens and sunshine anticipate the beauty of heaven, the upheavals of nature anticipate the suffering of hell. The New Testament gives us this warning, "Note then the kindness and the severity of God: severity toward those who have fallen, but God's kindness to you, provided you continue in his kindness" (Romans 11:22). We should not be surprised that nature is both kind and stern.

END-TIME CALAMITIES

Mercifully, Jesus gave us a preview, assuring us the full movie would eventually arrive in spectacular fashion. "There will be great earthquakes, and in various places famines and pestilences" (Luke 21:11). Let it not escape our notice that *pestilence* is listed among with the other judgments. Pestilence is defined as a contagion or infectious epidemic that is virulent and devastating. Is COVID-19 this predicted pestilence? No, I do not believe so, but it is a preview of a far worse pestilence that is still to come.

Jesus lists a number of signs and calls them "birth pains." For a mother, that means the baby hasn't yet been born but they're on their way. Be ready. The sorrows have begun, and the final judgment is about to begin, culminating with multitudes of people standing before the Judge of all the earth.

The death rate of COVID-19 perhaps was one percent of those who were infected; imagine pestilence and famine along with killings by a sword, which would wipe out 25 percent of the population! "And I looked, and behold, a pale horse! And its rider's name was Death, and Hades followed him. And they were given authority over a fourth of the earth, to kill with sword and with famine and with pestilence and by wild beasts of the earth" (Revelation 6:8). Added all together—pestilence, famine, killings—and you have massive number of people dying in the most excruciating ways. That's what yet awaits this cursed planet.

Those horrific plagues of locusts in East Africa are a preview of a coming locust invasion. After an angel is given the key to the bottomless pit we read,

> He opened the shaft of the bottomless pit, and from the shaft rose smoke. . . . Then from the smoke came *locusts* on the earth, and they were given power like the power of *scorpions* of the earth. They were told not to harm the grass of the earth or any green plant or any tree, but only those people who do not have the seal of God on their foreheads. They were allowed to torment them for five months, but not to kill them. . . . And in those days people will seek death and will not find it. They will long to die, but death will flee from them. (Revelation 9:2–6)

We must be careful when interpreting the symbolism of the book of Revelation. These locusts might be quite different than the pests we are acquainted with in this age. But what we cannot doubt is that they represent a terrifying judgment; a judgment well beyond any invasion of locusts we have seen on this planet. A desperate population will opt for suicide but will be unable to succeed; they have no choice but to remain alive though this horrific experience. These convulsions of nature will not be perceived as just the happenstance of "Mother Nature" but rather the judgment of "Father God."

Here is the terrifying description of the real movie, which will follow the preview.

When he opened the sixth seal, I looked, and behold, there was a great earthquake, and the sun became black as sackcloth, the full moon became like blood, and the stars of the sky fell to the earth as the fig tree sheds its winter fruit when shaken by a gale. The sky vanished like a scroll that is being rolled up, and every mountain and island was removed from its place. Then the kings of the earth and the great ones and the generals and the rich and the powerful, and everyone, slave and free, hid themselves in the caves and among the rocks of the mountains, calling to the mountains and rocks, "Fall on us and hide us from the face of him who is seated on the throne, and from the wrath of the Lamb, for the great day of their wrath has come, and who can stand?" (Revelation 6:12–17)

The description of other plagues and judgments to come are too numerous to list here.

The judgments that bring some people to repentance harden the heart of others. Anger toward God is the root of the worst possible rebellion.

Read this chilling account: "The rest of mankind, who were not killed by these plagues, did not repent of the works of their hands nor give up worshiping demons and idols of gold and silver and bronze and stone and wood, which cannot see or hear or walk, nor did they repent of their murders or their sorceries or their sexual immorality or their thefts" (Revelation 9:20–21).

If while reading this you have rebellion in your heart toward God, stop here and ask Him to create within you a sensitive and obedient heart. The hard truths of Scripture are not intended to drive us away, but to bring us near to God to accept His grace and mercy.

Let us remember the Bible speaks of a worldwide ruler, whom we call the antichrist, who will promise that all the world will be fed and fairness will demand that resources will be more equally distributed. He will come on a platform of peace, but when the time comes, he will insist on worldwide worship. And without his approval, people will starve.

In Revelation 13:16–17, we have this description of this evil dictator referred to as the beast, "Also it causes all, both small and great, both rich and poor, both free and slave, to be marked on the right hand or the forehead, so that no one can buy or sell unless he has the mark, that is, the name of the beast or the number of its name"

In years gone by this mark has been interpreted as some kind of a tattoo or indelible mark. But our present scenario can certainly be a picture of what's to come. This COVID-19 pandemic along with extensive technological advances, has given an opportunity for a global reset with increased surveillance and control. We have to wait and see the long-range effects of our present crisis.

Let us not be too hasty in thinking that we know when and how the end will come. In 2005, *The New York Times* carried the article "Doomsday: The Latest Word if Not the Last," in which it gave some examples of how quickly Christians rush to conclusions about the end of the world.[1] We heard the end was at hand when Israeli troops captured the Old City of Jerusalem in 1967, and later when Israeli Prime Minister Yitzhak Rabin worked out a peace accord with Yasser Arafat. And now we again hear from some preachers that the end of the world is near because of the growing number of natural disasters. I prefer to say much too little than a little too much.

We might not know *when* these things will happen; *that* they will happen is certain.

And even worse is yet to come.

HELL: THE GRAND FINALE

"Hell disappeared. No one noticed"[2] said historian Martin E. Marty. Hell may have disappeared from our theological radar screen, but it is clearly taught by Jesus and further explained and described in the book of Revelation.

On an airplane, I sat next to an older woman, and we struck up a conversation about religion, and at one point in the discussion, she said with an air of confidence, "If there is anything I know for sure, it's that hell doesn't exist." I replied somewhat wryly, "You know, you've put me in a really difficult dilemma because on the one hand I wish you were right. But on the other hand, Jesus mentioned *hell* at least eleven times. That's more than the number of times He mentioned *heaven*. So, either I have to go with you on this one, or I have to go with Jesus. Don't feel too hurt, *but I'm going with Jesus.*"

On these matters, like most others, personal opinions don't count. Instead of hardening our hearts and saying, "How could God do that?" we should open our hearts to receive what God says on the subject. Without faith in Christ and God's grace extended to us, the description we are about to read would be the experience of us all.

If God is willing to see people suffer on earth through pandemics, plagues, and natural disasters, why is it so hard to believe in hell? We already see at least an inkling of hell by watching the daily news.

A DESCRIPTION OF THE FINAL JUDGMENT

Read this passage carefully, and then I will attempt to explain its meaning:

> Then I saw a great white throne and him who was seated on it. From his presence earth and sky fled away, and no place was found for them. And I saw the dead, great and small, standing before the throne, and books were opened. Then another book was

opened, which is the book of life. And the dead were judged by what was written in the books, according to what they had done. And the sea gave up the dead who were in it, Death and Hades gave up the dead who were in them, and they were judged, each one of them, according to what they had done. Then Death and Hades were thrown into the lake of fire. This is the second death, the lake of fire. And if anyone's name was not found written in the book of life, he was thrown into the lake of fire. (Revelation 20:11–15)

This is the mother of all judgments. This is a judgment that is frightening, and yes, even terrifying. Imagine the scene. Think of tens of millions of people—perhaps billions—having to individually give an account of themselves to a holy God on that dreadful day, with nothing to shield them from His wrath. They stand destitute in the presence of His omniscience and omnipotence, and impeccable holiness and purity.

No one standing before Him will be able to tweak their record to make themselves look better. There will be no possibility of bribery or bartering for an out-of-court settlement; they will appropriately cringe in the presence of the sovereign, all-knowing Judge who will adjudicate with thoroughness. No hidden facts. No extenuating circumstances, just vivid truth and searing justice. All who appear here will intuitively know that this Judge administers justly.

We read that the great and small stood before God. John undoubtedly wants us to understand that this refers to people of different rank. A king is standing alongside those who died of poverty and sickness. Famous celebrities stand with the unknowns of this world; the wealthy stand with the poor. The aged stand alongside the younger generation. (I don't expect that children will be there, for they will be in heaven, as Jesus said, "their angels always see the face of my Father who is in heaven" [Matthew 18:10]).

What unites these diverse people and brings them together? They have this in common: they lack the kind of righteousness God demands for entrance into heaven. Human goodness cannot save them; only the gift of divine goodness could have qualified them for a heavenly entrance. As Paul assured the believers in his day, "Since, therefore, we have now been justified by his blood, much more shall we be saved by him from the wrath of God" (Romans 5:9).

The Time for Judgment

The judgment will be highly personal and individual. "Each one" will be judged according to their works. In order for it to be a just judgment, it must be a singular judgment, person by person. Each will have their moment before God. Not just what they did and said but the secrets of the heart will be laid bare (Romans 2:16). Motives will be examined to expose what they did or didn't do and why. The lies that were told, the cover-ups, the anger, the selfish, envious, and lustful thoughts and deeds—all these will be exposed. No one will debate with God because they will know intuitively that His record is painstakingly accurate.

Each person will be judged on the basis of what they did with what they knew based on their conscience, based on the light of nature, and based on whether or not they ever heard the gospel. "For all who have sinned without the law will also perish without the law, and all who have sinned under the law will be judged by the law" (Romans 2:12). He goes on to explain that the Gentiles, who do not have the revealed law (such as Israel had), will not be judged by the law but by the light of conscience (vv. 14–15). Israel, the nation that received the law at Sinai, will be judged by the standards of that law, whereas the pagans will be judged by the light of nature. Responsibility is based on knowledge. The one who knows God's ways will be punished more than the person who didn't. It will all be just.

Is God overreacting to their sin? Is their punishment greater than the crime? Sure, they sinned against God; yes, they did some evil things, but don't we all? In reply to this question, consider this: What if, as the theologian Jonathan Edwards believed, the greatness of the sin was dependent on the greatness of the person against whom it was committed? When I was a boy growing up on the farm, we kids would throw snowballs at one another. That was hardly considered worthy of a reprimand; but let's suppose you were to throw a snowball at the mailman, you might be in a bit of trouble. If you threw it at a policeman, that would be even more serious. If, however, you threw a snowball at the President of the United States, you would be arrested and jailed. The higher we go up the ladder of greatness and importance, the more culpability we have for our sin. Now think of the fact that all of our sins are against the holy, transcendent, pure, eternal, omnipresent, omnipotent God who created us. That makes even so-called "small sins" a serious infraction. Simply put, it is not possible to exaggerate how offensive our sin is toward God.

Why is the lake of fire eternal? All human beings will have been resurrected with eternal indestructible bodies and will therefore live somewhere eternally. Either we will be rejoicing in the presence of God or we will be in the lake of fire. The real you—the person you are—will live forever.

Those who have trusted Christ as Savior, while alive on Earth, "settled out of court." They took Jesus up on His promise, "For God so loved the world, that he gave his only Son, that whoever believes in him should not perish but have eternal life. For God did not send his Son into the world to condemn the world, but in order that the world might be saved through him" (John 3:16–17).

It is not too late for you to take advantage of what Jesus, in effect, says to us, "If you believe that My death was a sacrifice for sinners; if you believe that I bore your hell when I died on the cross; if you trust your eternal soul to

Me, you will be exempt from eternal punishment and you will be welcomed into the kingdom of My Father."

The "God" of liberal theology—the God who seeks the happiness of His creation to the best of His ability, the God who would never judge us for our sins or commit sinners to hell—does not exist in the Bible and is contradicted by the natural disasters and diseases in the world. The God of the Bible does not delight in human suffering, but He *does* delight in the triumph of truth and justice and the completion of His hidden purposes.

Let us bow humbly before the God who has revealed Himself in the Scriptures rather than a god we might prefer, a god of our imagination. We can thank COVID-19 for diverting our attention from this world to the world to come. And thank God we can avert the final judgment.

We should be eternally grateful that He has prepared a way of escape.

CHAPTER 7

GOD SAYS, "I HAVE PROVIDED A WAY OF ESCAPE."

Imagine, God speaks, and only a few listen.

"See that you do not refuse him who is speaking. For if they did not escape when they refused him who warned them on earth, much less will we escape if we reject him who warns from heaven . . . for our God is a consuming fire" (Hebrews 12:25, 29).

The greatest of all errors is to domesticate God, to believe that He is essentially like us only at a higher level. We forget that He is holy, hateful of sin, and jealous for His own glory. We forget that we could not possibly approach Him unless it is strictly on His terms and His appointed way. Two sons of Aaron, Nadab and Abihu, dared to come into God's presence dispensing with the proper protocol, and they were struck dead on the spot (Leviticus 10:1–3).

Just because people are not dying this way today doesn't mean that God has changed His mind about His holiness and hatred for sin. He waits patiently, but the end of all those who refuse His Son is an eternity of gloom and doom. No wonder we read, "It is a fearful thing to fall into the hands of the living God" (Hebrews 10:31).

Thankfully, God has provided a way of escape. By no means should the possibility of dying from COVID-19 be the greatest of our fears. To miss—or worse, to reject —the mercy that God offers is by far the greatest of all tragedies. We have a sin problem that is far worse than a COVID-19 problem. Sin is a virus that is universal, it infects every human being who has ever lived and those yet to be born, and it leads to eternal punishment. And for this virus, there is no human cure. Never has been, never will be.

We need a word of assurance, a word that gives us legitimate hope and peace. In short, we have to gladly accept the remedy God has provided. Thankfully, this cure is available to everyone. No one who comes to receive it on God's terms will ever be turned away.

TWO EARTHQUAKES, TWO REVELATIONS

There are two earthquakes—two natural disasters—that should especially attract our attention. Both teach us about God; both were accompanied by a revelation about the Holy One.

The first recorded earthquake in the Bible is when God gave the law at Mount Sinai. Let's put ourselves in the trembling sandals of the Israelites.

Now Mount Sinai was wrapped in smoke because the LORD had descended on it in fire. The smoke of it went up like the smoke of a kiln, and the whole mountain trembled greatly. And as the sound of the trumpet grew louder and louder, Moses spoke, and God answered him in thunder. (Exodus 19:18–19)

The mountain trembled because God wanted the people to stand in awe of His power and be appropriately afraid to approach Him carelessly. The voice of words spelled out the content of the moral law; the voice of nature spelled out His power and authority. The Ten Commandments shouted His rules for living; the trembling mountain was shouting His reasons for our worshipping. To fear Him was not only appropriate, but commanded.

God told the Israelites, in effect, "Stay back!" If you even touch an animal that has touched the mountain you will be killed (Exodus 19:13). These instructions had to be meticulously obeyed. God was revealing His glory and the right to be obeyed. And the people were appropriately terrified.

Thank God that centuries later, there was another earthquake. This earthquake coincided with the dying of Jesus just outside of the walls of Jerusalem. "And behold, the curtain of the temple was torn in two, from top to bottom. And the earth shook, and the rocks were split" (Matthew 27:51). Also terrifying, but filled with hope.

The timing of the earthquake at Sinai and the earthquake at Calvary could not have been more precise. Two earthquakes, two acts of revelation, and two judgments. On Mount Sinai, God spoke the law with its inflexible demands and warned of disobedience; on Calvary God spoke words of kindness and mercy through the sacrifice of Jesus, because He was judged for our sins.

Both events were accompanied by the shaking of the earth; both tell us something about God. And both remind us that when God speaks, the mountains and rocks tremble.

From Sinai to Calvary

These two events are given an interesting interpretation in the book of Hebrews. The writer makes a contrast between the Old Covenant where God shook the earth at Sinai, and the New Covenant, which was instituted at Calvary. I began this chapter with the first of these verses, now let me quote them in context.

See that you do not refuse him who is speaking. For if they did not escape when they refused him who warned them on earth, much less will we escape if we reject him who warns from heaven. At that time his voice shook the earth, but now he has promised, "Yet once more I will shake not only the earth but also the heavens." This phrase, "Yet once more," indicates the removal of things that are shaken—that is, things that have been made—in order that the things that cannot be shaken may remain. (Hebrews 12:25–27)

We've learned that twice the earth was shaken when God revealed Himself. The first was at Sinai, the second was at Calvary, but there is a third yet to come when everything that can be shaken will be shaken so that only the unshakable will remain.

And now the conclusion: "Therefore let us be grateful for receiving a kingdom that cannot be shaken, and thus let us offer to God acceptable worship, with reverence and awe, for our God is a consuming fire" (vv. 28–29).

The final natural disaster will split the world into two separate kingdoms: the unshakable kingdom of God and the disintegrating kingdom of the damned. It is almost too frightening to visualize. I described it briefly in the preceding chapter.

The worldwide COVID-19 pandemic vividly reminds us that life is short and the triumph of God over this world is certain. There is a time coming when everything that has been nailed down will be torn up. And in the final judgment, the whole earth will be destroyed and be recreated by God and only what then remains will be eternal.

Now comes an invitation for all who are fearful, weary, and aware they need to be rescued from their sins. This is God's most blessed provision for needy people just like us. *The judgments of Mount Sinai were borne by Christ on Mount Calvary.*

COME TO CALVARY

There is a reason why the author of Hebrews describes both Mount Sinai and Mount Calvary. The terror of God was averted because Jesus bore it for all who would believe on Him. The wrath of Sinai is transformed into the grace of Calvary.

Unbelievers must live both now and forever under the judgment of Sinai; believers live both now and forever under the mercy and grace of Calvary. Same God, same attributes, same need for justice. Jesus made the difference. He bore the curse that belonged to us.

Let these promises bless our weary hearts:

There is therefore now no condemnation for those who are in Christ Jesus. (Romans 8:1)

Whoever believes in the Son has eternal life; whoever does not obey the Son shall not see life, but the wrath of God remains on him. (John 3:36)

Jesus "delivers us from the wrath to come." (1 Thessalonians 1:10)

For God has not destined us for wrath, but to obtain salvation through our Lord Jesus Christ, who died for us so that whether we are awake or asleep we might live with him. (1 Thessalonians 5:9–10)

Since, therefore, we have now been justified by his blood, much more shall we be saved by him from the wrath of God. (Romans 5:9)

Christ redeemed us from the curse of the law by becoming a curse for us—for it is written, "Cursed is everyone who is hanged on a tree." (Galatians 3:13)

Anne Ross Cousin, the wife of a Free Church of Scotland pastor, wrote this hymn that vividly describes the fact that Jesus bore what we deserved; He paid for the guilt of sin that belonged to us.

> O Christ, what burdens bowed Thy head!
> Our load was laid on Thee;
> Thou stoodest in the sinner's stead,
> Didst bear it all for me.
> A Victim led, Thy blood was shed;
> Now there's no load for me.
>
> Death and the curse were in our cup:
> O Christ, 'twas full for Thee;
> But Thou hast drained the last dark drop,
> 'Tis empty now for me.
> That bitter cup, love drank it up;
> Now blessing's draught for me.[1]

When we come to Sinai and experience the holiness of God, we flee to Calvary to experience the grace of God. Sinai fills us with terror; Calvary fills us with acceptance and mercy. The only protection from the terrors of Sinai is the canopy of grace given to us at Calvary.

Sometimes God shouts and sometimes He whispers. If He will not be heard in natural disasters and pandemics, perhaps He will be heard in the quietness of our souls. Perhaps we will take the time to ponder His mercy and heed the warnings He has given, through Jesus Christ our Lord.

Today is the day of salvation. We do not know when the end will come, but when it arrives, it will be too late to prepare for the grand finale.

"Therefore, stay awake, for you do not know on what day your Lord is coming. But know this, that if the master of the house had known in what part of the night the thief was coming, he would have stayed awake and would not have let his house be broken into. Therefore you also must be ready, for the Son of Man is coming at an hour you do not expect." (Matthew 24:42–44)

Blessed are those who respond to the uncertainties of this life as a reminder to prepare for the certainties to come. Many years ago I was speaking in California and we were told that Frank Sinatra's grave was in a cemetery nearby. With the help of an iPhone, we found it quite quickly and discovered that written on his tombstone was the title of one of his favorite songs, "The Best Is Yet to Come." I am not Frank Sinatra's judge, for judgment belongs to God. But we can say with confidence that if he did not take advantage of the redemption and protection that Jesus Christ offers us, for him "The Worst Was Yet to Come."

Sobering.

AVOIDING THE FINAL CURSE

To recap: Jesus bore the Last Judgment for all who believe on Him. When we receive Him as our sin-bearer, we are given the gift of His righteousness so that we can be welcomed into God's presence and declared righteous. But only Jesus is qualified to prepare us for eternity because He was not just a teacher, but a *Savior*.

Back in the days when homesteaders were on the prairies, they would frequently light a fire around their homes at a time when the wind was calm. They knew that prairie fires that started in the distance could head their way if a fierce wind blew the flames toward them. But when they prepared their land with a "controlled burn," they burned as much grass and weeds as they could around their homes, knowing they were safe because *they were living where the fire had already been.*

Just so, when we transfer our trust to Jesus, we are standing where the fire of God's judgment has already come. Let me repeat this promise and the warning, "Whoever believes in the Son has eternal life; whoever does not obey the Son shall not see life, but the wrath of God remains on him" (John 3:36). "Let us offer to God acceptable worship, with reverence and awe, for our God is a consuming fire" (Hebrews 12:28–29).

SAVED OR LOST?

Natural disasters, pandemics, and plagues *do* divide the human race between the dead and the living. The dead have no opportunity to repent, no second chance at life and redemption. "And just as it is appointed for man to die once, and after that comes judgment, so Christ, having been offered once to bear the sins of many, will appear a second time, not to deal with sin but to save those who are eagerly waiting for him" (Hebrews 9:27–28).

Recall that the RMS Titanic went under with 1,522 people going to a watery grave. Even if we attribute the sinking to a series of human errors, God most assuredly was able to keep the ship from sinking without any violation of the human will. This is another reminder that the God who permits such unthinkable tragedies is one who is to be feared.

After the news of the tragedy reached the world, the challenge was how to inform the relatives whether their loved ones were among the dead or the living. At the White Star office in Liverpool, England, a huge board was set up; on one side was a cardboard titled Known to Be Saved, and on the other, a cardboard with the words, Known to Be Lost. Hundreds of people gathered to watch the signs. When a messenger brought new information, the question was: to which side would he go?

Although the travelers on the Titanic were embarked as first, second, or third class, after the ship went down, there were only two categories: the rescued and the drowned. Just so, we can divide people into many different classes, based on geography, race, education, and wealth. But in the final day of judgment, there will be only two classes:

the rescued and the lost. There is only heaven and hell.

Perhaps in heaven a mother will be looking for her son, wondering if he will arrive safely behind the pearly gates. Wives will wait for husbands, and parents for children. Today is a day of grace, a day of waiting for the living to repent.

If you have never come to saving faith in Christ, do it now. Acknowledge your sinfulness and your need to be rescued by Christ Jesus. Accept the fact that He bore your sin and took the punishment that you deserve. Transfer your trust to Him in an act of repentance and faith. Receive His gift of righteousness believing His promise to receive all who come to Him, "But to all who did receive him, who believed in his name, he gave the right to become children of God" (John 1:12).

Let me say it one more time: only Jesus is qualified to "deliver us from the wrath to come." He is a great Savior, for great sinners.

CHAPTER 8

WE SAY, "WE WILL WITNESS WITH WORKS AND WORDS."

How do we reach out to those who are suffering? And what do we say when asked about God's role in tragedy? What we don't do is come with a list of ready answers, slickly packaged and ready for distribution. We do come with hearts filled with sympathy and hands ready to help. We are to be witnesses for Christ, pointing people beyond themselves to biblical hope.

Where do we begin?

WE MUST GRIEVE

We must begin any discussion of tragedy by grieving for those who are in pain. Many of us are better at trying to explain the whys and wherefores of pandemics and disasters than we are weeping over them! An entire book of the Old Testament describes in vivid detail the grief that the prophet Jeremiah experienced at the devastation of Jerusalem. No doubt most of the people were disobedient, disregarding God's warnings. But likely there were also many God-fearing people who were killed or starved to death in the siege. Jeremiah recognizes that even when the cruel Babylonians came, God was in charge; it is He who inflicted the judgment, but yet the prophet weeps, just as we should.

Jeremiah writes as though the city herself is speaking:

"Is it nothing to you, all you who pass by?
    Look and see
if there is any sorrow like my sorrow,
    which was brought upon me,
which the LORD inflicted
    on the day of his fierce anger.

"From on high he sent fire;
  into my bones he made it descend;
he spread a net for my feet;
  he turned me back;
he has left me stunned,
  faint all the day long. . . .

"For these things I weep;
  my eyes flow with tears;
for a comforter is far from me,
  one to revive my spirit;
my children are desolate,
  for the enemy has prevailed."
(Lamentations 1:12–13, 16)

Jeremiah models for us a blending of human compassion and solid theology; yes, *God* brought the judgment upon the people; He used evil people to destroy Jerusalem. But the prophet is not angry with the Almighty, nor does he stoically accept suffering because it was deserved. He grieves over the ruined city. He laments the fact that the people were so disobedient they invited punishment.

Disasters cause us to pause, they cause us to ask hard

questions, and if we care about the world, they drive us to tears. Can anyone stare at the destruction of an earthquake or the devastation of a worldwide pandemic and not weep? Surely a heart of human compassion takes the time to identify with the loss, the suffering, and the hopelessness of fellow human beings. We should not approach disasters with an accusatory finger or a detached attitude. Grieving hearts can only be touched by other grieving hearts, sharing pain and mingling tears.

Any answer must begin with personal compassion and a heavy heart.

Tears, if they are not wasted, should lead to deeds. The church is called to suffer and to die with the world, and nowhere is that more necessary than when tragedy strikes. Some believers suffer because they are caught in the tragedy itself; others suffer because they are willing to sacrifice for others. I commend those who are willing to leave the comforts of home and bring hope and healing to the victims. Not all of us can go, but all of us can give; we can participate in helping relief agencies as they try to bring hope to those who are so utterly destitute. When disaster strikes, the church should be the church!

God wants us to release our grip on our money, our

resources, and our selfishness. When disasters come, we should be the first to respond with sacrifice and generosity.

We begin with grief and then we seek for understanding.

WE MUST GIVE THANKS

Any catastrophe should remind us of all of the blessings we take for granted; it should lead us to deep and lasting gratitude. Before we ask why so many die in natural disasters or due to an epidemic, we should ask a different question, "Why are so many people—we included—*still living*?" How many people who are angry with God never give Him thanks for beautiful weather and the numerous benefits that nature regularly bestows upon this planet?

Every day that we live with sunshine, food, and health—these are gifts we don't deserve. God multiplies many blessings for both the righteous and the unrighteous: "But I say to you, Love your enemies and pray for those who persecute you, so that you may be sons of your Father who is in heaven. *For he makes his sun rise on the evil and on the good, and sends rain on the just and on the unjust*" (Matthew 5:44–45).

And so the sun shines to warm us, the rain falls to

bless us, and the stars shine to remind us that God is not only in heaven, but also on earth to give us mercies we don't deserve. We should be grateful for the times when the earth is firm, when the tornadoes are gone, and when the floods subside. The same book of Lamentations that describes the grief of Jeremiah says, "The steadfast love of the LORD never ceases; his mercies never come to an end; they are new every morning; great is your faithfulness" (Lamentations 3:22–23).

Life is a gift and God has the right to give it and take it. Often the same people who ask where God was when a disaster happens thanklessly refuse to worship and honor Him for experiencing years of peace and calmness. They disregard God in good times and think He is obligated to provide help when bad times come. The God they dishonor when they are well should heal them when they are sick; the God they ignore when they are wealthy should rescue them from impending poverty; and the God they refuse to worship when the earth is firm should rescue them when it begins to shake.

Let us freely admit that God owes us nothing. Before we charge God with not caring, let us thank Him for those times when His care is very evident. We should pause and realize we are surrounded by undeserved blessings. Even in His silence, He blesses us.

WE MUST GRACIOUSLY RESPOND TO SKEPTICS

How do we dialogue with honest skeptics?

The argument of skeptics can easily be stated: if a God who is omnipotent, omniscient, and loving existed, He would do away with evil and suffering. Since horrendous suffering exists, He must either be weak, unknowing, or sadistic. Since such a God does not commend our respect, atheism seems to be a more attractive alternative. Atheists therefore look about, see the misery millions endure, and ask sarcastically, "Where was God when COVID-19 spread around the world, leaving people dead and families starving?" And they defy anyone to give an answer.

The question coming from an atheist is illegitimate and irrational. To ask such a question is to assume the existence of God. If there were not a creator God—if we are but a complicated combination of atoms that sprung into existence randomly—then the very idea of good and evil or better and best could not exist. After all, according to atheists, atoms have arranged themselves blindly according to haphazard patterns and whatever is, just *is*.

So, if the atheist/naturalist asks where God was in a disaster, he is assuming a moral framework that can only exist if God exists. Remember, on atheistic premises, there can be no spiritual substance such as soul or mind, only patterns of physical particles. Naturalists are in the unhappy position of having to maintain that matter can think; that molecules can ask questions about which arrangement of matter is good and which is bad. Clearly, notions about good or evil cannot arise from the atoms that existed in primordial slime.

C. S. Lewis makes the same point when he argues that only God can account for the moral law that exists in all of us. He says that in his atheistic days, he argued against God because the universe appeared so cruel and unjust. Then he realized that his idea of justice presupposed a standard that was beyond himself; he continues,

Of course I could have given up my idea of justice by saying it was nothing but a private idea of my own. But if I did that, then my argument against God collapsed too—for the argument depended on saying that the world was really unjust, not simply that it did not happen to please my private fancies. Thus in the very act of trying to prove that God did not exist—in other words, that the whole of reality was senseless—I found I was forced to assume that one part of reality— namely my idea of justice—was full of sense.[1]

Lewis goes on to argue that the moral law is a better reflection of God than the universe itself. He points out that the intuitive knowledge that we have of good and evil tells us more about God than nature does: "You find out more about God from the Moral Law than from the universe in general just as you find out more about a man by listening to his conversation than by looking at a house he has built."[2]

In an atheistic world, evils can never serve a higher purpose and suffering can never be redeemed, for it can never lead to nobler ends. Suicide would be attractive, for there would be no point in staying around to make this world a better place because in the end, everyone dies and goes out of existence. Furthermore, the injustices of this world will never be answered.

A Jewish friend of mine, who is an atheist, admitted that he felt some disquiet of spirit to know that Hitler would never be judged for what he did. He has no hope that there will be a final adjudication to set the record straight. He ruefully admitted that without eternity, the events of time can never be redeemed or made right.

Atheism satisfies neither the mind nor the heart. And yet atheists do ask questions about good and evil for one reason: they also are created in the image of God and have a soul that can think. Ravi Zacharias said that a relativist may say God has died, "but the questions from his soul at a time like this reveal that he cannot kill Him completely."[3]

An Answer for a Defiant Repairman

"If there is a God and I go to hell, I will defy and curse Him forever." That's what a repairman said to me when he was in our home fixing some electrical problem. He spoke for many who have either turned to atheism or skepticism because of the suffering of this world. They argue that a good, omnipotent God would put an end to this madness.

How do we respond?

What I told him was this: "I see your point, and you

can retreat into your atheism/skepticism if you wish, but consider this . . . if the biblical God exists, and He does have the power to put an end to evil but doesn't, it's clear that God is to be feared. No wonder the Bible says, 'It is a fearful thing to fall into the hands of the living God,' and we should tremble in His presence because we also read, 'our God is a consuming fire.' Walk away from Him if you wish, but you do that at your own eternal peril. If you think a tsunami brings horrendous suffering, far worse eternal suffering awaits you in the life to come. God is who He is, and we can't change Him to make Him more appealing to our preferences."

I challenged him to make a better choice. Come to the protection that He has provided in Jesus Christ. He was sent to die for us, and He spares us from the wrath to come (Romans 5:9; 1 Thessalonians 5:9). His death and resurrection provided atonement for those who believe on Him. God's anger against sinners was appeased when Christ died on the cross; but this blessing only comes to those who admit their sin and their need for a Savior— someone who is actually qualified to present us to God on His behalf—to present us to God as spotless, perfect to be welcomed by the Father. Jesus alone can do this for us, "I am the way, and the truth, and the life. No one comes to the Father except through me" (John 14:6).

My point: why fight against a wrathful God, when you can be embraced by Him in love and become a son or daughter of the Almighty forever? Think of how quickly He turns from wrath to unconditional love because of Jesus. Already in the Old Testament we have this invitation, "Kiss the Son, lest he be angry, and you perish in the way, for his wrath is quickly kindled" (Psalm 2:12).

My experience has been that atheism almost always grows out of anger, deep resentment, and hurt. Perhaps anger against religious but abusive parents; or deep hurt done by a judgmental church, or anger against God for unanswered prayer. So we must be patient, loving, and good listeners. Yet we must let people know it would be terrible if their attitude were to keep them from embracing the hope Jesus offers us.

We all agree that this earth is not the best of all possible worlds, but from the standpoint of eternity, the best of all architects chose the best of all possible blueprints. This does not mean that God is pleased with evil; it means that He is pleased with how He will use it toward wise and good ends.

WE MUST CHOOSE

Let's tell our friends that pandemics and natural disasters force us to decide how we will respond to God. We can accuse Him, or worship Him, but neutrality is impossible. When disasters strike, God is not on trial, *we are.*

We owe a debt to COVID-19, to earthquakes and hurricanes that vividly remind us that life is short and Christ's return is certain. Tragedies teach us to hold unto Christ tightly and everything else loosely.

Meanwhile we serve, we help, we risk, and we care. And we tell people that our only hope is Christ: "For to me to live is Christ, and to die is gain" (Philippians 1:21).

With our works and our words, we want to glorify God. "In the same way, let your light shine before others, so that they may see your good works and give glory to your Father who is in heaven" (Matthew 5:16). The world needs the witness of God's people more than ever.

And by His grace we will continue to believe despite times of doubt.

CHAPTER 9

WE SAY, "LORD, WE BELIEVE; HELP OUR UNBELIEF!"

We live by promises, not explanations.

Wars, poverty, natural disasters, disease, and horrendous injustices exist on this planet. Who can possibly calculate the buckets of tears that are shed at any given hour in this fallen world? Can we trust a sovereign God who could, at any moment, put an end to such suffering? A God who could have prevented the catastrophes that have pounded the world throughout the centuries? A God who could have had Hitler die as an infant in his mother's arms?

An intellectual answer—even a true one—never satisfies the human heart. Grief is never removed by a word about God's eternal and transcendent purposes. And yet, we are encouraged to respond to God, for as Ecclesiastes 3:11 tells us, God has put eternity in our hearts.

We can learn from those who are an inspiration to our faith; heroes who believed the Scripture even in the face of contrary evidence. We are inspired by those who believed we don't have to know everything about God's purposes to believe in His goodness and comfort.

A STORY OF FAITH
AND HOPE DURING A PLAGUE

Martin Rinkart was a Lutheran pastor in Ellenberg, Germany, back in the seventeenth century. This was at the beginning of what is called the Thirty Years' War, and his town became a focal point in the battle. Soldiers came and went, often living in the town in crowded conditions. In 1637, a terrible plague came to Ellenberg, and Rinkart was the only pastor alive, so he presided over all of the funeral services. The estimate is that 4,000 died in one year.

Rinkart gave leadership, sometimes burying fifty people in a day in joint funeral services.

Yet it was in those dark times that he wrote the hymn,

> Now thank we all our God
> with heart and hands and voices,
> who wondrous things have done,
> in whom his world rejoices;
> who from our mothers' arms
> has blessed us on our way
> with countless gifts of love,
> and still is ours today.

Here is a man who was able to give thanks to God in the midst of devastation, untold grief, and many unanswered questions. He never lost sight of the fact that God reigns and is to be praised even in the midst of uncontrolled sorrow.

> O may this bounteous God
> through all our life be near us,
> with ever joyful hearts
> and blessed peace to cheer us,

to keep us in His grace,
and guide us when perplexed,
and free us from all ills
of this world in the next.

All praise and thanks to God
the Father now be given,
the Son and Spirit blest,
who reign in highest heaven
the one eternal God,
whom heaven and earth adore;
for thus it was, is now,
and shall be evermore.[1]

What would you do if you had God's power for twenty-four hours? Of course, we'd all answer that we would rid the world of poverty, war, disease, and disasters of every type. We would put an end to all forms of evil and create a paradise for all. *If only!*

On the other hand, if we were also given God's wisdom, I'm convinced that we would leave things as they are! For our all wise and all powerful heavenly Father has a hidden agenda that makes sense out of it all.

There is meaning in the madness.

However—and this is important—if we ask the next question as to what God's ultimate, hidden purpose is in these devastating events, then we can only say that He is relentless in the pursuit of His own glory (Jeremiah 13:11; 2 Thessalonians 1:9–10). Enough has been written in this book to show that we have some insight into the divine mind, but let us humbly confess that we see only glimpses of God's eternal purpose.

After years of reading and thinking about the problem of reconciling the suffering of this world with God's mercy, I have concluded that there isn't a solution that will satisfy the mind of a skeptic—especially a dishonest skeptic. God's ways are "past finding out." He has simply not chosen to reveal all the pieces of the puzzle. *God is more inscrutable than we care to admit.*

After all the theological essays have been written, after all of the debaters have become silent, we still won't understand; we have no choice but to stand in awe of great mystery. John Stackhouse has written,

The God of predestination, the God of worldwide providence, the God who created all and sustains all and thus ultimately is responsible for all—this God has revealed to us only glimpses of the divine cosmic plan. God has not let us see in any comprehensive way the sense in suffering, the method in the madness. God has chosen, instead, to remain hidden in mystery.[2]

Yes, God has chosen to remain a mystery.

In his book, *On First Principles*, the influential church father Origen of Alexandria, Egypt (AD 185–254), described what the apostle Paul meant when he wrote that God's judgments are "unsearchable" and His ways "unfathomable." Read these words:

Paul did not say that God's judgments were hard to search out but that they could not be searched out at all. He did not say that God's ways were hard to find out but that they were impossible to find out. For however far one may advance in the search and make progress through an increasing earnest study, even when aided and enlightened in the mind by God's grace, he will never be able to reach the final goal of his inquiries.[3]

God really meant what He said: "'For my thoughts are not your thoughts, neither are your ways my ways,' declares the LORD. 'For as the heavens are higher than the earth, so are my ways higher than your ways and my thoughts than your thoughts'" (Isaiah 55:8–9). We should stand in awe of both the mystery and the wonder of His ways.

I am thankful that *it is not necessary for us to understand the hidden purposes of the Almighty in order to believe that such purposes exist*. If we believe only when we understand, our faith is small; when we believe even when we don't understand, such faith brings glory to God. Yes, someday we might be granted the ability to understand. "For now we see in a mirror dimly, but then face to face. Now I know in part; then I shall know fully, even as I have been fully known" (1 Corinthians 13:12). We see the jumbled bottom of the tapestry, only God sees the pattern from above.

In a previous chapter we quoted Paul's words: "For I consider that the sufferings of this present time are not worth comparing with the glory that is to be revealed to us" (Romans 8:18). In the future, the unseen will give meaning to that which is seen. Eternity will interpret what happened in time. Meanwhile *we live by promises, not explanations*.

A PERSONAL ANSWER

Where do we turn when the ambiguity of God's ways overwhelms us? Martin Luther, in pondering the mystery of God's ways, urged us to flee the hidden God and run to Christ. Now, of course, the "hidden God" and the God who was made flesh are one and the same; they are not separate divinities from which we must choose.

But as Stackhouse points out, it is precisely because the two are one that Luther's advice works. He writes, "One must run away from the mysteries of God's providence about which we cannot know enough to understand (because God has revealed so little about them), and run toward Jesus Christ in whom we find God adequately revealed."[4] God assures us in His Word that He is for us and that nothing shall separate us from His love.

Look at the world today, and we might never think that God loves us and cares. Or at least, we could argue that God's attributes are ambiguous: at times caring, at other times indifferent and callous. We would not know whether God intended to punish us at the end of life or forgive us. Just read the history of philosophy and you will agree that no coherent idea of God can ever be formed on the basis of observation and experience.

If we want to discover whether God cares about His creation, we have to look beyond this world to His revelation. It is there we find hope that we could never discover on our own, "For God so loved the world, that he gave his only begotten Son, that whosoever believeth in him should not perish, but have everlasting life" (John 3:16 KJV).

In his book, *The Silence of God,* Sir Robert Anderson wrestles with the apparent indifference of God to human pain and tragedy. After asking all the important "why" questions, he writes the following that deserves a careful reading:

But of all the questions which immediately concern us, there is not one which the Cross of Christ has left unanswered. Men point to the sad incidents of human life on earth, and they ask, "Where is the love of God?" God points to that Cross as the unreserved manifestation of love so inconceivably infinite as to answer every challenge and silence all doubt forever. And that Cross is not merely the public proof of what God has accomplished; it is the earnest of all that He has promised. The crowning mystery of God is Christ, for in Him "are all the treasures of wisdom and knowledge hidden." And those hidden treasures are yet to be unfolded. It is the Divine purpose to "gather together in one all things in Christ." *Sin has broken the harmony of creation, but that harmony shall yet be restored by the supremacy of our now despised and rejected Lord.*[5]

Anderson goes on to say that it was in the power of these truths that the martyrs died. Heaven was as silent then as it is now. There is a report that when some Christian martyrs were marched to their death in France, they sang so loudly the authorities hired a band to drown out the sound of their hymns. No sights were seen, no voices heard, no deliverance granted. And yet they believed that God was with them.

Speaking of similar martyrdoms, Anderson comments, "But with their spiritual vision focused upon Christ, the unseen realities of heaven filled their hearts, as they passed from a world that was not worthy of them to the home that God has prepared for them that love him."[6] Facing persecution and death they found comfort in Jesus.

God's Love Toward Us Remains

All too often we read the promises of God too quickly. Read this promise thoughtfully: "For I am sure that neither death nor life, nor angels nor rulers, nor things present nor things to come, nor powers, nor height nor depth, nor anything else in all creation, will be able to separate us from the love of God in Christ Jesus our Lord" (Romans 8:38–39). Just think of what Paul is saying: no pandemic, plague, or natural disaster that overtakes us can ever separate us from God's love.

Clearly, God has not chosen to deliver us from these tragedies. But, rather, He has chosen to grant us grace to go through such trials without explanations. We are not guaranteed deliverance from disaster, but promised His presence as we go through such trials. John Piper calls COVID-19 "a bitter providence" but says that the believer can find sweetness in it, *"knowing that the same sovereignty that could stop the coronavirus, yet doesn't, is the very sovereignty that sustains the soul in it.* And not only sustains, but sees to it that everything, bitter and sweet, works together for our good—the good of those who love God and are called in Christ (Rom. 8:28–30)."[7]

To His disciples who were about to be bereft of their

leader, and who would later die for their faith, Jesus gave this assurance. "Let not your hearts be troubled. Believe in God; believe also in me. In my Father's house are many rooms. If it were not so, would I have told you that I go to prepare a place for you? And if I go and prepare a place for you, I will come again and will take you to myself, that where I am you may be also. And you know the way to where I am going" (John 14:1–4).

To quote Stackhouse once more, "We can respond properly to evil in our lives because *we know that God is all-good and all-powerful because we know Jesus.*"[8]

Questions about the mystery of evil are not solved in this life but in the next. "So we do not lose heart. Though our outer self is wasting away, our inner self is being renewed day by day. For this light momentary affliction is preparing for us an eternal weight of glory beyond all comparison, as we look not to the things that are seen but to the things that are unseen. For the things that are seen are transient, but the things that are unseen are eternal" (2 Corinthians 4:16–18).

Yes, ultimately the strength of our faith will be dependent on the One in whom we have come to trust. We can face the uncertainty and trials of life with optimism, helping others along the way. "We can . . . know Jesus, and in his embrace, we can in turn embrace the suffering world and offer it a sure hope."[9]

Why doesn't our heavenly Father care for us as a good earthly Father would—responding to our requests and shielding us from the plagues of this fallen world? The answer is that our Father loves us more than our earthly father could possibly love us, but He has a different set of priorities. We value health, and so does our Father; but He values our faith even more. He delights in providing food for us, but He delights even more when we trust Him though we are hungry or even starving to death. And yes, He delights when we trust Him even when He seems to be absent when we need Him the most.

Matthew Henry wrote, "God often hides himself in the darkness, but never far away." C. S. Lewis, in imagining the lead demon, Screwtape, tells the demonic underling, Wormwood, "Do not be deceived, Wormwood. Our cause is never more in danger than when a human, no longer desiring, but still intending, to do our Enemy's will [God's will], looks round upon a universe from which every trace of Him seems to have vanished, and asks why he has been forsaken, and still obeys."[10]

What if God wanted to set up a series of circumstances to prove that some people will go on trusting Him, even in the midst of pain, and in the absence of clear explanations? What if our faith means so much to the Almighty that He is willing that we suffer if only to prove our devotion and love, even when so much evil in the world counts against His love and care?

The children weeping because of drought, disease, and starvation—terrible though it is, is not the last chapter in the history of this world. Skeptics are unconvinced, but those of us who have met our Savior are convinced that He both knows and cares. We are also convinced that the last chapters of the book He is writing will someday clarify the meaning of the earlier smudged paragraphs. Corrie ten Boom who herself endured the horrors of a Nazi Concentration Camp is believed to have said, "Never be afraid to trust an unknown future to a known God."

You might remember the story about a blotch of black paint that was spilled randomly on a canvas. A creative artist decided to paint a beautiful landscape working the black paint into the picture. What appeared to be destructive became a part of a larger, more perfect design. In the end, every injustice will be answered; suffering will be redeemed, and God's glory will be displayed.

A HOPE THAT IS
SURE AND STEADFAST

"I'll tell you, I have no hope. I see no hope for the world."

Those are the words of Sir Winston Churchill to Billy Graham when they met after Graham's 1954 Greater London Crusade. Churchill opined that the headlines were filled with murder and the possibility of war. Communism, he said, might conquer the world. Then he asked more personally, "I am a man without hope. Do you have any real hope?" [11]

That's the question everyone is asking: Do we have *real* hope?

If COVID-19 has taught us anything, it's that we can't predict the future. Who would have dreamed that a virus would be so contagious that it would kill hundreds of thousands around the world and result in our economy being shut down? Professional sports, restaurants, and businesses closed. Airlines grounded and millions unemployed. There are as many dire situations as there are people reading this.

Turn anywhere and you will find blogs and sermons that tell people to "just trust God." Fair enough. But what does that mean? That the economy will be restored? That those who are unemployed will be rehired? That those who are ill will get well? That we will come out on the other side of this "stronger than ever"?

Not necessarily.

We need a hope that can withstand setbacks, personal losses, and unanswered prayers. We need a hope that endures when the pain is unending and the future is growing progressively darker. "Trusting God" does not mean things will be better. Just ask Jesus as He agonizes in Gethsemane.

So, what is the basis of our hope? Hope, as understood in the Bible, is not, "I hope everything will turn out okay, but I'm unsure." Scriptural hope is "confident expectation." It means we have something to look forward to; and it is something that we can depend on.

Let's meditate on this promise that we "might have strong encouragement to hold fast to the hope set before us. We have this as a sure and steadfast anchor of the soul, a hope that enters into the inner place behind the curtain, where Jesus has gone as a forerunner on our behalf, having become a high priest forever after the order of Melchizedek" (Hebrews 6:18–20).

Here hope is described as a refuge disconnected from circumstances. During the COVID-19 crisis many of us learned to "shelter in place." But we also have to learn that "He who dwells in the shelter of the Most High will abide in the shadow of the Almighty" (Psalm 91:1). I grew up singing a hymn in church titled, "A Shelter in the Time of Storm," that reminds us that we need a refuge, a shelter that is impervious to the stock market or even our own health, important as those may be. It is unaffected by tonight's news or tomorrow's headlines. This does not mean that when we flee to this refuge, all of our worries will be gone; peace is a gift that has to be accepted, but it also has to be won. Even as we flee to our refuge, we may still fret. But we also learn that we have an invisible friend who has gone before us and meets with us in the secret place.

This "refuge" is not a physical place; it is a hope that resides within us, "a sure and steadfast anchor of the soul." Our body is important, but not supremely important; our circumstances are important, but not supremely important. But our soul is where life makes up its mind; it is the captain of our ship and the means by which we connect to the invisible world.

Hope does not guarantee that life will get easier; hope is the assurance that God will be with us whether it will get easier or not. Hope does not mean that we will be healed; hope means that God is with us in our sickness and even in death. Hope does not promise a change in circumstances; it promises a change of heart. Our faith is best demonstrated not when things are going well but when they are not going well.

Jesus is our forerunner. In ancient times, "forerunner" referred to a person who would jump from a boat, swim to shore, and then by means of a rope and a primitive winch, guide the boat to its landing without it being destroyed against the rocks. We look to Jesus who is already "behind the curtain" (Hebrews 6:19), the One who arrived ahead of us. He has seen it all, endured it all, and won it all. And now He cheers us on as our companion, guide, and intercessor. Why did He run His race? He did it for the "joy" set before Him. No joy in Gethsemane; no joy being whipped; no joy on the cross—but He endured by looking beyond the present to the future.

On the morning of July 4, 1952, Florence Chadwick

waded into the water on Catalina Island and began swimming toward the coast of California. She wanted to be the first woman to swim the 21-mile strait, but the fog was so thick that she could hardly see the boats in her own party. More than fifteen hours later, her mother and her trainer in a boat alongside her urged her to go on, but she said she simply couldn't and was taken out of the water. Moments later, when she saw that she was within a half mile from the shore, she said, "If I could have seen the shore, I would have made it." Two months later, despite heavy fog, she made it and said that as she swam, she kept a mental image of the shoreline in mind.[12]

Let's agree to look beyond the fog to the shore. The journey may be treacherous, but our destination is sure. Darkness comes before light, and resurrection after crucifixion. Like our Master, we run the race with an eternal goal in mind. He made it safely to heaven and now He stands ready to welcome us. When Stephen was being stoned, he already saw Jesus waiting.

During this conversation with Churchill, Billy Graham took out his New Testament and explained to Churchill that he too could have hope, but he had to look beyond the London headlines to Christ. Just so, let us watch the news tonight to get caught up on what's going on in the world; but if we want real hope, we have to look beyond this world to the next.

Jesus waits for us behind the curtain and assures us that with His help, we can make it. He made it and so can we. Meanwhile, we serve Him, for as long as He wills. As Calvin put it so eloquently, "For we unjustly defraud God of his right, unless each of us lives and dies in dependence on his sovereign pleasure."[13]

Yes, we serve at His sovereign pleasure. And when He calls our name, we will join Him behind the curtain.

DEALING WITH DOUBT

After John the Baptist was thrown into prison, he began to have second thoughts as to whether or not Christ was the Messiah. For one thing, the Old Testament predicted that when the Messiah came, the prisoners would be freed (Isaiah 61:1). John made the same error as those who believe God is obligated to heal us today: he misinterpreted the timing and application of some of God's promises.

As long as John sat in the dungeon, it seemed that Christ was reneging on the promises of God found in

Isaiah. And, I'm sure he reflected on how unfair it was that he, who had played such a vital part in Christ's earthly ministry, should be so summarily punished for taking a righteous stand against Herod's sinful marriage. So, John sent a delegation to Christ to pointedly ask: "Are You the Expected One, or shall we look for someone else?" (Matthew 11:3 NASB). He was polite, but he was hurting badly. Jesus had disappointed him.

In response, Jesus reminded John that miracles were being done and then added, "Blessed is he who does not take offense at Me" (v. 6 NASB). We could paraphrase, *"Blessed is the person who is not upset with the way I run my business."*

Blessed is the person who does not say, "After the suffering I saw as a result of an earthquake, I will never believe in God again." Blessed is the person who does not say, "I am never going to trust God because He didn't keep me from injustice and abuse. Or from COVID-19."

Blessed is the person who understands that we must trust God's heart when we cannot understand His hand; blessed is the person who knows that we must stand in awe in the presence of the mystery of God's purposes.

Blessed is the person who keeps on believing no matter what. Blessed is the person who lets God be God.

Remember, *birds sing not because they understand, but because they have a song.*

A MOTHER
WHO WAS READY
FOR THE BIG ONE

Almost every time I visit California, someone is talking about earthquakes, and many residents are expecting "the big one" that could destroy most of Los Angeles and the surrounding areas. For years, geologists have known that the San Andreas Fault, a line that runs near the coast, is vulnerable to a massive shaking, an earthquake that could dwarf all others experienced so far.

But the really "big one" will not be confined to California; it will encompass the whole earth. When Christ comes to wrap up history as we know it, this earth, cursed as it is by sin, will burn with fire, and God will remake it according to His specifications.

We've talked about the shaking of the earth, but the universe itself is spoken of as disappearing, or at least being destroyed in a giant inferno and recreated. Nothing we have ever read or seen will compare with this:

But the day of the Lord will come like a thief, and then the heavens will pass away with a roar, and the heavenly bodies will be burned up and dissolved, and the earth and the works that are done on it will be exposed. Since all these things are thus to be dissolved, what sort of people ought you to be in lives of holiness and godliness, waiting for and hastening the coming of the day of God, because of which the heavens will be set on fire and dissolved, and the heavenly bodies will melt as they burn! But according to his promise we are waiting for new heavens and a new earth in which righteousness dwells. (2 Peter 3:10–13)

The conclusion follows:

"Therefore, beloved, since you are waiting for these, be diligent to be found by him without spot or blemish, and at peace" (v. 14).

In the final destruction of the cosmos, all that will be remain is God, the devil, angels, and people. And yes, the present earth will be recreated; there will be a new heaven and a new earth, and eternity will officially begin. Such a massive destruction is still in the future; but if we are ready for the natural disasters of today, we will be ready when the big one comes.

Let me share the story of a young mother who was ready.

When the devastating earthquake hit Haiti back in 2010, approximately 220,000–300,000 people were killed.[1] The suffering was horrendous; homeless children, many of them newly orphaned, were roaming through the rubble seeking a bit of food and someone to care for them. It was enough to make a stone weep.

Of all the images that come to mind when I think back to that horror, I see in my mind a young mother with a baby in one arm and her meager possessions in another, getting ready to board a bus to take her to some unknown shelter where she hoped to be cared for.

A reporter stepped close to her to ask about what happened to her in the devastated town.

She replied, "I lost my son. He died in the rubble. He was only eighteen months old."

"Did you get to bury him?"

"No, no chance, his body was crushed in the rubble; I just had to throw him away."

Just then I noticed the camera zeroed in on her backpack and stuffed in a side pocket was a Bible. Then, she said, "God is our refuge and strength, an ever-present help in trouble . . ." Her voice trailed off as she got onto the bus and disappeared from view.

When the report was over, I just kept staring at the television for a moment pushing back tears and letting what I'd just seen sink into my soul. A dead child, a baby in her arms, boarding a bus that was going she knew not where; no chance to plan a funeral and pay respects to her precious little one, and there she was still believing, still trusting that God was her refuge and strength.

This mother—God bless her—began quoting Psalm 46, which was written as a praise song when God spared the city of Jerusalem during the invasion of the Assyrians who were threatening to annihilate the inhabitants. In the midst of a harrowing escape, the people found God to be an unshakable pillar.

Let's read the first three verses: "God is our refuge and strength, a very present help in trouble. Therefore we will not fear though the earth gives way, though the mountains be moved into the heart of the sea, though its waters roar and foam, though the mountains tremble at its swelling."

God is our refuge. A refuge, a shelter, a safe place where you run when everything else is disintegrating around you. God is unaffected by the fluctuation of events of earth; He is always there, solid, unmoved. When the mountains are tottering into the depths of the sea, and the ground beneath you is shaking, when we run to God He will be there for us.

No wonder the Psalm ends, "Be still, and know that I am God" (v. 10). Even in adversity, He is there; or perhaps I should say *especially in adversity* He is there! Let us cease striving and let God be God.

Revered Henry F. Lyte was a pastor in Scotland who battled tuberculosis most of his life. On his final Sunday, September 4, 1847, amid many tears, the congregation sang "Abide with Me," a song he himself had composed. It spoke of the unchanging God in an ever-changing world.

Abide with me: fast falls the eventide;
the darkness deepens; Lord, with me abide.
When other helpers fail and comforts flee,
Help of the helpless, O abide with me.

Swift to its close ebbs out life's little day.
earth's joys grow dim, its glories pass away.
Change and decay in all around I see.
O Thou who changest not, abide with me.

. . . .

Hold thou thy cross before my closing eyes.
Shine through the gloom and point me to the skies.
Heaven's morning breaks and earth's vain shadows flee;
in life, in death, O Lord, abide with me.[2]

The young mother clutching an undernourished baby in her arms, with no time to mourn the tragic death of her other child, found solace in the God who was still with her when the earth gave way. "God is our refuge and strength," she said amid her grief and tears. With that kind of faith, God is highly honored and pleased. Eternity will vindicate her and prove her faith to be "more precious than gold" (1 Peter 1:7).

"For the sufferings of this present time are not worth comparing with the glory that is to be revealed to us" (Romans 8:18). Put all of the weight of our trials on one side of the scale and the glory that awaits us on the other. The scale will go plunk! Eternity will give meaning to time. His presence today, His glory tomorrow.

Here is a personal prayer you can adopt and adapt as you wish.

A PRAYER

Father in heaven, I worship you for the mystery of your ways. I confess that I don't understand or fathom the hidden purposes you have in human suffering. Yet, as sinners we know that we are being judged in many different ways because we have dishonored your glory. But I thank you that Jesus died to remove the curse, so that I can be shielded from your holy anger against my rebellion. I thank you that because of the gift of Jesus' righteousness I am your son/daughter forever. For I accept the promise, "But to all who did receive him, who believed in his name, he gave the right to become children of God, who were born, not of blood nor of the will of the flesh nor of the will of man, but of God" (John 1:12–13). Thank you that whether I live or die, I am yours. And I pray in Jesus' name, Amen.

Be encouraged: Our King is on His way.

ACKNOWLEDGMENTS

Thanks to the entire team at Moody Publishers for working together to see this book become a reality in record time! You believed in this message and encouraged me along the way. And thanks to Tyndale House Publishers for graciously giving me the rights to a previous publication titled *Where Was God?* in which I grappled with God's role in natural disasters. My freedom to repurpose parts of that work gave me a head start in responding to the COVID-19 phenomenon.

Duane Sherman, your phone call asking about the possibility of my writing a book like this sparked a fire within my bones that this message of God's sovereignty in the midst of nature's fury had to be written. And, Amanda

Cleary Eastep, once again as my editor, you challenged some of what I had written and helped me tweak the message in places where it needed tweaking! Also, thanks to Michael Pitts of Moody Church who suggested the subtitle, *What Is God Saying to Us?*, which helped me organize the chapters.

Erik Peterson, your design and logistical skills have made this book "welcoming" to a wide audience; and thanks to Jeremy Slager and the entire marketing and sales force determined to let the public know that the book is available! And let me acknowledge faithful servants such as Arthur Eastern, along with his team, who work behind the scenes making sure that Moody books are distributed into the hands of those who need them! God will reward you!

Finally, to my lovely wife, Rebecca. Thanks for your encouragement as I again spent many hours at my computer to complete this project. "Many women have done excellently, but you surpass them all" (Proverbs 31:29). Those words were written to describe you! Thanks, my love!

Most importantly, all praise goes to Jesus, our Lord, our Savior and coming King!

NOTES

Chapter 1: The Crisis That Changed Everything

1. Scott Pelley, "Coronavirus and the Economy: Best and Worst-Case Scenarios from Minneapolis Fed President," CBS News, March 22, 2020, https://www.cbsnews.com/news/coronavirus-and-economy-best-and-worst-case-scenarios-60-minutes-2020-03-22.

2. Serena Gordon, "Coronavirus Pandemic May Lead to 75,000 'Deaths of Despair' from Suicide, Drug and Alcohol Abuse, Study Says," CBS News, May 8, 2020, https://www.cbsnews.com/news/coronavirus-deaths-suicides-drugs-alcohol-pandemic-75000.

3. Neha Wadekar, "Two New Generations of Locusts Are Set to Descend on East Africa Again—400 Times Stronger," Quartz Africa, April 10, 2020, https://qz.com/africa/1836159/locusts-set-to-hit-kenya-east-africa-again-400-times-stronger.

4. Andy Crouch, Kurt Keilhacker, and Dave Blanchard, "Leading Beyond the Blizzard: Why Every Organization Is Now a Startup," The Praxis Journal, March 20, 2020, https://journal.praxislabs.org/leading-beyond-the-blizzard-why-every-organization-is-now-a-startup-b7f32fb278ff.

5. John Keats, Poetical Works and Other Writings, vol. 4 (London: Reeves & Turner, 1883), 107.

Chapter 2: The Silence of God

1. William H. McNeill, *Plagues and Peoples* (New York: Anchor Books, 1976), 122.

2. Quoted in Rodney Stark, *Exploring the Religious Life* (Baltimore: The Johns Hopkins University Press, 2004), 37.

3. Timothy F. Lull, ed., *Martin Luther's Basic Theological Writings* (Minneapolis: Augsburg Fortress Publishers, 1989), 744.

4. Ibid., 742.

5. Thomas Downing Kendrick, *The Lisbon Earthquake* (Philadelphia: J. B. Lippincott Company, 1957), 137.

6. See, e.g., Jenny Rose Spaudo, "Cindy Jacobs Calls Christians across World to Pray against Coronavirus," *Charisma*, March 7, 2020, http://www.charismamag.com/spirit/prayer/44610-cindy-jacobs-calls-christians-across-world-to-pray-against-coronavirus.

7. T. B. Joshua, "Since yesterday, when the Lord brought the revelation about the rain and that this rain will wipe away the epidemic coronavirus," Facebook, March 2, 2020, https://www.facebook.com/tbjministries/posts/3028260480628041, and "CORONAVIRUS PROPHECY UPDATE," Facebook, March 10, 2020, https://www.facebook.com/tbjministries/photos/a.105659106221541/3046000355520720/?-type=3&theater.

8. T. B. Joshua, "CORONAVIRUS PROPHECY!!!," Emmanuel TV, March 2, 2020, YouTube video, 20:48, https://www.youtube.com/watch?v=iAlpIRY4FTs.

9. Shawn Bolz, "The Lord showed me The end of the Coronavirus . . . the tide is turning now!," Facebook, February 28, 2020, https://www.facebook.com/ShawnBolz/posts/10163544765850657.

Chapter 3: God Says, "I Am in Charge, Trust Me."

1. James Dalrymple, "The Lost and Helpless Flee from Hell to the Hills," *Independent,* August 26, 1999, https://www.independent.co.uk/news/world/the-lost-and-helpless-flee-from-hell-to-the-hills-1115390.html.

2. Tony Campolo, "Katrina: Not God's Wrath—or His Will," BeliefNet, January 8, 2006, https://www.beliefnet.com/faiths/christianity/2005/09/katrina-not-gods-wrath-or-his-will.aspx.

3. Isaac Watts, "I Sing the Almighty Power of God," Representative Text, Psalter Hymnal, 1987, https://hymnary.org/text/i_sing_the_mighty_power_of_god.

4. John Piper, *Coronavirus and Christ* (Wheaton, IL: Crossway, 2020), 42, https://document.desiringgod.org/coronavirus-and-christ-en.pdf?ts=1586278809.

5. John Piper, "Whence and Why the Earthquake in Turkey?" *DesiringGod*, August 18, 1999, https://www.desiringgod.org/articles/whence-and-why-the-earthquake-in-turkey.

6. William Cowper, *The Complete Poetical Works of William Cowper*, ed. H. S. Milford (London: Oxford University Press, 1913), 455.

7. Quoted in Charles Swindoll's *The Mystery of God's Will* (Nashville, TN: W Publishing Group, 1999), 115.

Chapter 4: God Says, "There Are Lessons You Should Learn."

1. Dave Miller, "God and Katrina," Apologetics Press, August 5, 2005, http://www.apologeticspress.org/apcontent.aspx?category=12&article=1556.

2. Max Lucado, "What Harvey Can Teach Us," August 29, 2017, https://maxlucado.com/harvey-can-teach-us/.

3. James Houston, ed., *The Mind on Fire—An Anthology of the Writings of Blaise Pascal* (Portland: Multnomah, 1989), 51.

4. Katie Benner, "Mark Zuckerberg and Priscilla Chan Pledge $3 Billion to Fighting Disease," *New York Times,* September 21, 2016, https://www.nytimes.com/2016/09/22/technology/mark-zuckerberg-priscilla-chan-3-billion-pledge-fight-disease.html.

5. C. S. Lewis, "The Screwtape Letters," *The Complete C. S. Lewis Signature Classics* (New York: HarperOne, 2002), 198.

6. Ibid.

7. Ibid.

8. Piper, *Coronavirus and Christ*, 66.

Chapter 5: God Says, "You Live in a World That Is Under Judgment."

1. Piper, *Coronavirus and Christ*, 56.

2. Ibid., 36.

Chapter 6: God Says, "The Worst Is Yet to Come."

1. Michael Luo, "Doomsday: The Latest Word If Not the Last," *New Your Times,* October 16, 2005, https://www.nytimes.com/2005/10/16/weekinreview/doomsday-the-latest-word-if-not-the-last.html.

2. Martin E. Marty, "Hell Disappeared. No One Notices. A Civic Argument," *Harvard Theological Review* 78, no. 3–4 (October 1985): 381–98, https://doi.org/10.1017/S0017816000012451.

Chapter 7: God Says, "I Have Provided a Way of Escape."

1. Anne R. Cousin, "O Christ, What Burdens Bowed Thy Head," https://hymnary.org/text/o_christ_what_burdens_bowed_thy_head.

Chapter 8: We Say, "We Will Witness with Works and Words."

1. C. S. Lewis, *Mere Christianity*, in *The Complete C. S. Lewis Signature Classics* (New York: HarperOne, 2002), 41.

2. Ibid., 34.

3. Ravi Zacharias, "The Silence of Christmas and the Scream of the Tsunami," *RZIM,* https://www.rzim.org/read/just-thinking-magazine/the-silence-of-christmas-and-the-scream-of-the-tsunami-soul-speak-in-a-suicidal-culture.

Chapter 9: We Say, "Lord, We Believe; Help Our Unbelief!"

1. Martin Rinkart, "Now Thank We All Our God," 1636, https://hymnary .org/text/now_thank_we_all_our_god.

2. John G. Stackhouse Jr., *Can God Be Trusted?—Faith and the Challenge of Evil* (Downers Grove, IL: InterVarsity, 2009), 117.

3. Origen, *On First Principles* (New York: Harper and Row, 1966).

4. Stackhouse Jr., *Can God Be Trusted?*, 118.

5. Sir Robert Anderson, *The Silence of God* (Grand Rapids, MI: Kregel, 1952), 150–51. Emphasis added.

6. Ibid., 152.

7. Piper, *Coronavirus and Christ*, 50.

8. Stackhouse Jr., *Can God Be Trusted?*, 120.

9. "Tsunamis and Birth Pangs," *Christianity Today*, January 13, 2005, https://www.christianitytoday.com/ct/2005/february/4.28.html.

10. Lewis, *The Complete C. S. Lewis Signature Classics* (New York: HarperOne, 2002), 208.

11. Billy Graham, *Just As I Am* (San Francisco: Harper, 1997), 236. See also: BGEA, "Billy Graham Trivia: Which World Leader Asked Billy Graham for a Last-Minute Meeting?" Billy Graham Evangelistic Association, June 27, 2017, https://billygraham.org/story/billy-graham-trivia-what-world-leader-did-billy-graham-have-a-secret-meeting-with/#.

12. Randy Alcorn, "Florence Chadwick and the Fog," Eternal Perspective Ministries, January 21, 2010, https://www.epm.org/resources/2010/Jan/21/florence-chadwick-and-the-fog.

13. John Calvin, "CCCCXXI.—To Richard Vauville," November 1555, in *Letters of John Calvin*, vol. 1, comp. and ed. Jules Bonnet (Eugene, OR: Wipf & Stock, 2007), 236.

Epilogue: A Mother Who Was Ready for the Big One

1. "Haiti Earthquake Fast Facts," CNN, December 12, 2013, updated June 2, 2020, https://www.cnn.com/2013/12/12/world/haiti-earth quake-fast-facts/index.html.

2. Henry Francis Lyte, "Abide with Me: Fast Falls the Eventide," 1847, https://hymnary.org/text/abide_with_me_fast_falls_the_eventide.

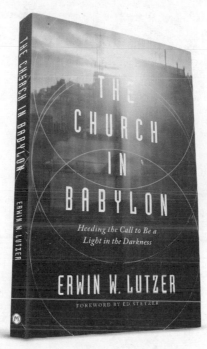

GET THE RESOURCES YOU NEED FOR WHEN LIFE TAKES AN UNEXPECTED TURN.

978-0-8024-2332-0   978-0-8024-2338-2   978-0-8024-2341-2   978-0-8024-2343-6

978-0-8024-2344-3   978-0-8024-2345-0   978-0-8024-2359-7   978-0-8024-2360-3

Be it in the midst of a natural disaster, global unrest, or an unforeseen pandemic, the repercussions of unprecedented change can leave us all reeling. Get the wisdom, encouragement, and peace you need to ease your anxieties, strengthen your relationships, and encounter the almighty God during such trying times.

also available as eBooks

MOODY
Publishers®

From the Word to Life®